LIVING OFF THE GRID

A How-To-Guide for Homesteading and Sustainable Living

Written by
Bo Morgan
Kathy Campbell

After the Power Goes Out
due to...

Extended Power Outage?

Electric Company Disconnect?

Self-Sufficiency Enthusiast?

Possibility Adventurer?

Shoestring Budget?

Share in our experience learning:

How to Inexpensively Live

Off the Electricity Grid

Table of Contents

Introduction

In this book are all the best tips, tricks and techniques on how to inexpensively live off the grid.

They were all tried and tested during our real-life experiences when a relatively minor problem caused our power to go out unexpectedly for over a year.

This is the story of how we survived without electricity, unprepared, and learned to work with what we had on a small budget.

We share these experiences with you to give you the encouragement and confidence to live through your own unique off-grid experience.

You're going to get through this. Many people have.

We did and we will tell you exactly how!

"The life which men praise and regard as successful is but one kind."
— Henry David Thoreau, Walden

This book is for anyone who finds themselves short of money when the power goes out or those who just want the thrill and challenge of living off-grid.

This book is NOT about how to expensively convert your home to solar, wind or water power. It is NOT about how to gracefully go off-grid if you can afford to invest the thousands of dollars needed to set up your home with batteries and accessories to generate and store alternative energy.

We romantically researched going off-grid permanently with an alternative power system, concluding that we could not afford it yet. This book is for others who find themselves in similar situations.

You can use the information in this book to help you achieve self-sufficiency. You can research solar, wind, water, pedal and wind-up technologies and explore alternative ways of doing things that rely on electricity. This book is about how to manage your home through an extended power outage. It just might change your life.

We are a husband and wife who live in a rural Canadian farmhouse which we are fixing up slowly. Our farmhouse experience may seem cushy because in many ways it is a beautiful place to live, but we still faced all the challenges of living without electricity in below freezing temperatures, feeding ourselves and washing our clothes, dishes and bodies. We learned:

- How to get clean without a hot shower

- How to deal with laundry, cooking and finding enough power to continue to run our internet-based business from home

- How to get water when our electric water pump didn't work and our car broke down preventing us from driving to our local spring

We experienced this as a husband and wife team, but even if you are a single woman or a parent, you can do this! I want to emphasize that even though my husband and I both helped keep the house going, with the right items, preparedness and tools, a woman need not feel that this text, this book and the information contained in it do not apply to her. Women on their own, men on their own and whole families with children can live and thrive off-grid.

However, there may be regulations where you live which prohibit living without electricity, especially in condos and rental units. Your home's insurance policy might not allow a wood stove. If you have close neighbors, running a noisy generator might be a problem for them and earn you a visit from the police. You or a family member may have health issues that require the convenience of electricity. We urge you to carefully consider the risks and effects on everyone involved.

Because it will not be easy.

Not at first anyway.

There will be many challenges **and dangers**, which we will attempt to warn you about with red highlights throughout this book, so proceed with **caution**.

Be Safe!
Off-grid, you take responsibility for yourself.

"When you first jump, your parachute will not open right away. I'm sorry. I wish I could tell you it does but it don't. If you jump, it's not going to open up right away. You're gonna hit them rocks and you're gonna get some skin tore off on them cliffs. You're gonna get all your clothes torn off. You're gonna get some cuts on you. You're gonna be bleeding pretty bad but eventually… EVENTUALLY the parachute has to open."

- Steve Harvey, comedian

After 13 months, we finally went back on-grid, mainly because solar power is not cost-efficient. Also, full-time, whole-house generators require too much fuel to operate 24/7, and they still require a dependency on the fossil fuel supply chain, which is just a different kind of "grid."

We learned that currently (no pun intended), electricity is so expensive that subsidies are in place to make it more affordable for consumers. Solar could start receiving that same attention. Sadly though, solar is hard to harvest in many geographic areas and requires the use of expensive, heavy, toxic storage batteries that must be replaced every few years.

This book is not about how to convert to solar, though we hope to someday. Instead, we'll show you how to use a mix of affordable means, like portable generators, gas stoves and heaters, and newer means such as wind-up and rechargeable devices. This is a book about how to live, thrive and survive when the power suddenly goes out, because that's what happened to us.

We also did not want to have to resort to getting day jobs just to come up with the huge sum to get our house's electricity back up and running. We love the home-based business we have been running for a few years now, which we continued to run throughout our off-grid experience. We are glad to report that we pulled through and continue to live our life of freedom, working from home and enjoying our wonderful old farmhouse, built when the electricity grid did not yet exist. Too bad the original wood stove and water well have been removed - that would have made things MUCH easier!

Are you ready for this? I want to show you what we discovered about how the average person can find new freedom for themselves when the power goes out.

In this book, we will show you:

- *How to begin planning today for your off-grid experience*

- *How to deal with all the essential aspects of living a normal life when a power outage catches you by surprise*

- *How to work from your off-grid home and make your own income*

- *And much more!*

Thanks again for purchasing this book. We hope you find it inspirational!

Chapter 1
Electricity

You've Got the Power... Oh Wait, You Don't

When we had sudden needs for immediate repairs to our old farmhouse's electrical system, we did not have five thousand dollars to get back on track immediately, so we decided to give off-grid life a try. Without electricity, basic things we used to take for granted were not there anymore.

It was one of the hardest (and best) things we've ever done. The first need was for at least enough electricity to get our computers and internet running. We run a home-based business and have no other income, so a minimum amount of electricity was crucial to work, earn and save our way out of this situation. Additionally, the internet is an incredible resource that came in handy many times throughout the experience.

In the beginning, we only had our car and an old, dead Noma Powerpack that we had leftover from our previous house that used to back up a basement sump pump. The Noma Powerpack is an 1800W backup power device that plugs into regular 115V wall power and charges up a battery pack inside under normal circumstances. When the power goes out, the battery pack converts power through a built-in inverter to supply 115V power (up to 1800 watts) to five three-prong outlets. It's useful for powering a basement sump pump when rainstorms knock out the power.

However, our unit was about ten years old and the battery pack was completely dead. Upon removing the panels, we found that the battery pack consisted of three small ATV batteries, all of which were swollen, and one split open. No wonder they wouldn't take a charge anymore!

Necessity is the mother of invention and desperate times call for desperate measures, so we invented our own little hack. There were no YouTube videos to guide us through this one. We took the panels off the Powerpack and carried it outside to the driveway. We took car battery booster cables and connected the dead Noma battery terminals to the running engine (positive to positive, negative to car chassis/ground), and turned the Noma pack on. It worked!

Noma Backup Power System wired for car power

Connecting booster cables to a car battery can be dangerous. Know what you are doing and be careful.

We ran a 100-foot extension cord from the Noma in the driveway into the house and plugged in our power bar. We were able to get about 1000 watts out of it before the Noma shut itself off automatically, beeping with an error code. A run to the driveway to press the power button turned it back on. It was converting our car's alternator power to more than enough energy to recharge four of our laptops, a AA battery charger, an office lamp, a mobile phone, an internet modem and a Wi-Fi router.

As long as we kept the motor running, it only cost us gasoline to have enough power to run our business and maintain our connection to the outside world. We never ran the Noma pack off the car without the engine running. This would have run the risk of depleting the car battery, leaving us stranded, or at least the with hassle of finding someone to give us a boost. We were always careful and it never happened, but having to run the car engine constantly wasn't always convenient or inexpensive.

The Noma battery numbers were printed clearly and an internet search showed that our local automotive supply store had them in stock for $80 each. We bought one to start and it worked fine. In addition to powering all our devices, the car also recharged the single Noma battery back to full in about an hour. When we disconnected the Powerpack to turn the car off, it automatically switched into battery backup mode, and that single battery continued to provide enough power for an additional hour. By that time the laptops were charged and we had already been online for an hour, so we could switch the Powerpack off and save that hour for later when the various device batteries were run down again. For $80 we doubled our power time!

The daily experience of this power generation technique taught us an important (and costly) lesson. ALWAYS secure the hood of the vehicle after every use. Unfortunately, we did not close the hood tight one evening. The next morning we rushed out the door to the local public pool for a luxurious hot shower and swim. We didn't notice the hood was still ajar, and as soon as we revved up to speed it flipped open and smashed the windshield.

Secure the hood of the charging vehicle after every use.

This was a terrifying experience that thankfully was not much worse, plus another expensive $500 repair that we hadn't budgeted for. It added yet another immense challenge to our already difficult situation.

At least the broken windshield did not prevent us from running the engine in the driveway to power our little Powerpack inverter. This allowed us to continue to run our home-based business from home, rather than having to visit a library or coffee shop with Wi-Fi every day. This was our main concern, that we could continue the lifestyle of freedom that we have come to enjoy with our home-based business.

The Powerpack also allowed us to run one light bulb in our main work area for a few hours. What a comfort! While we ran the car to juice up the power pack, we were able to connect to the internet to check email a few times per day and surf the net to see what news, messages and job leads there were. It also gave us a chance to download any entertainment that we wanted to watch, but we always had to conserve our computer power as much as possible. If we downloaded a two-hour movie, we might not have had enough power to watch the whole thing. Or, more importantly, we might not be able to finish an important project for one of our clients.

Being able to do this was the cornerstone of our decision to continue the off-grid lifestyle until we could afford to make the electrical repairs we needed to. That was in October. We had no idea then that it would take over a year!

During this time, we had to collect our water in jugs at a local spring. Four months later, the Canadian winter grew colder and collecting water from the spring became painfully cold, and dangerously icy and slippery. We realized that the Powerpack wasn't enough and we were going to need more power to jet pump water from our drilled well and keep the house and ourselves from freezing.

We listed a few items for sale on the online classifieds and raised the money we needed to purchase a second-hand portable generator for $400, which was delivered on New Year's Day. It was a Coleman Powermate 5000 with a 10hp Tecumseh motor connected to an electric motor gen-set that boasted 5000 watts of continuous running power, 6250 watts for short peaks and had both 120 and 240V outlets. Even though we never got quite that much power out of it, it did generate enough to recharge the Noma Powerpack and run the furnace, hot water tank, water pump, refrigerator, lights and computers simultaneously.

Coleman Powermate 5000, portable generator

A two-hour generator session was enough to refill our water jugs and check the internet while the water tank heated up, then take a couple of showers, do some dishes, run the washing machine (but not the clothes dryer - this was always a problem) and recharge all our devices. We discovered we could even run the hair dryer after our shower, but only in ten-second hot bursts, then ten-second cold bursts before the next hot burst, without stalling the generator. We stalled the generator plenty of times trying to figure out exactly what we could get away with, each time requiring a run outside (in the snowy winter) to restart it with its pull cord.

Pulling ripcords can cause shoulder injuries.

It would usually start right away. If it didn't, it needed five minutes to cool off before it would, no matter how hard or how often we pulled the cord. It became important to not overdo it and hurt our shoulders by pulling the start cord too much, making it even more important not to stall it in the first place.

The power company had severed our power lines from the house mast and removed the meter as a "safety disconnect," so our house was completely cut off from the grid. This gave us the freedom to wire the generator directly to our fuse box, and we removed the fuses we didn't need and the fuses for the high draw items like the fridge, water pump and hot water heater. Once the generator was fired up, we had to be careful of the order in which we plugged these high draw fuses back in to avoid stalling the generator. The fuse for the hot water heater put a huge strain on the generator, so we made sure nothing else was running when we plugged that one back in.

Connecting a generator to a fuse box is dangerous and illegal.

Under normal circumstances, it is irresponsibly **dangerous** and **illegal** to connect a generator directly to a fusebox. This is because the generator power can back-feed, that is, go backward into the grid's utility power lines, and **injure or possibly even kill an unsuspecting powerline worker** conducting routine maintenance.

Since we were not connected to the grid's utility power lines at all, there was zero risk of this happening, but the electricians and inspectors who saw our setup were clearly uncomfortable with the idea and refused to reconnect the power until the generator was safely disconnected from the fuse box. Understandable!

The generator ended up requiring quite a bit of regular maintenance and tuning up, but nothing we couldn't do for ourselves, especially with all the handy troubleshooting guides available online for this popular model. We had to clean the carburetor of the gummy residue left from old gas (we used a spray can of quick-start to dissolve it), and there was a tuning screw that kept vibrating loose and causing the motor to surge and run horribly, but it was easy enough to secure it in place with a bent clip. Other than that, it needed regular oil changes after every 25 hours of use, which can be messy, and it takes a heavy grade of oil (SAE30, not the usual 10W30 that cars use).

Twice it stopped generating electricity even though the motor was still running, and we traced the fault to a circuit board in the gen-set called an automatic voltage regulator (AVR). The first time we were able to solder a small piece of copper wire into a circuit that had burnt out. It was a relatively easy fix that cost nothing. The next time the AVR went bad it was a little blue diode that broke off, probably from all the vibration, and since we could not find the missing diode we ended up buying a new AVR board from a local electrician for about $100. The diode showed up months later and it looked fine, just broken at the stems.

That Coleman generator lasted us over eight months of daily use, running it at least two hours every day. Then in August, it made a loud bang and an awful clacking sound and died. It had thrown its piston rod and smashed the cast aluminum side wall of the motor wide open. There was no way to fix this.

Amazingly, we found another Coleman Powermate for sale that had never (or rarely) been used but would not start for $100. All we wanted were the parts, but when we brought it home, we found the carburetor was thoroughly gummed up with evaporated gasoline. Our old carb was clean as a whistle, so we were able to make a quick swap of the carburetor parts, and the new Coleman fired right up and ran beautifully. We used it for another couple of months until the power company switched us back on again.

Well, almost. As previously mentioned, we had to disconnect the generator from the fuse box for the final week for the electrician and utility company to safely reconnect the fuse box to the grid power lines.

In terms of making the home livable and being a patient troubleshooter and fixer of problems, you'll do well if you have an "every challenge is an opportunity" attitude.

"I've lived a slower and less expensive life going off the grid, and I'm happier because of it."

- Ed Begley, Jr.

Chapter 2
Water

Collecting and Use

We have our own home with a private, drilled water well, but without electricity, we can't get the water out of it. We thought a manual hand pump, like the kind you see in the old days of the Bonanza TV series, might work. However, it would have been a large expense, since our well is drilled quite deep, and would have required a serious pump. Besides, we weren't sure that we wanted to stay off-grid. This made our water supply a bit iffy and limited to the few hours per day we were able to power our generator to pump water... as long as the water pump didn't break down. And, of course, it did.

Although we had wondered about the off-grid world we had never intentionally turned our main power switch off just to try it. Who does?

We did not have any alternative way to run our appliances, including the water pump, until we got the used generator on New Year's Day. Until then, for a little over two months, we were not able to use our home's electricity to obtain any water, heat, refrigeration or anything else, except a light, the internet and our computers. These essentials allowed us to continue to work from home using our car's engine for battery power and the Noma Powerpack as an inverter to run the computers, internet and a lamp.

For about nine weeks the water pump was useless to us and we couldn't get water out of our well. We are fortunate to know of a couple of nearby roadside freshwater springs where you can fill up your own jugs with as much lovely, mountain-fresh spring water as you can carry. This is how we got all our water for the first two months we lived off-grid. Every few days, we drove to the spring and filled up as many jugs and other containers as we could hold in the back.

Spring water must boil for ten minutes before drinking.

Boiling water won't remove pollution like chemical pesticides or automotive fluids. There can be chemical toxins in the water caused by such things as leaching, road runoff and other factors. These kinds of impurities in the water **cannot** be removed by boiling and can be harmful to you and your family, pets and visitors, so please be sure the water you will be using or consuming does not contain chemical pollution. If it does, then it is not useable and you will need to find a different water source.

We used this water for everything - drinking, cooking, bathing, cleaning, doing dishes, etc. This worked out well for us for a while. The water from the spring is fantastic. Though locals say you can drink it raw, whenever cooking or drinking the water directly, we boiled it for ten minutes to ensure purity and prevent illness. We don't want to take any chances with our health and well-being; it's not like we can call in sick. We must stay able-bodied enough to collect and carry water, etc. So, we added factory-bottled spring water to our regular grocery list for drinking cold. At about a dozen jugs per week, the growing number of empties were useful for carrying even more fresh spring water on each visit; we went about twice per week. Having enough clean jugs that don't leak is a big deal when you need to transport water for drinking, cooking, cleaning, and flushing.

You face many unexpected and last-minute challenges when you're off-grid. It's significantly harder to make and keep everything clean, so hygiene is of utmost concern. Cleaning and sanitizing things as often as possible is important. You don't need the added challenge of illness so it's important to do things like boil any raw water that you plan to drink, which works for us because other than water our favorite drinks are hot coffee and iced tea, which you need to boil water for anyway.

For a while, we went on like this, and it was a fun privilege to visit these beautiful natural springs so often. We felt fortunate to be out there experiencing something that we would not have if we had been glued to our computers, which was usually the norm.

The downside was that we had to manually lift and carry **a lot** of water and it was hard on our backs and shoulders. Plus, as mentioned previously, when the Canadian winter set in, it became uncomfortably cold to fill jugs under the splashing waterspout of the freezing cold spring, even with rubber gloves.

Even with those considerations, however, we were doing okay with the "getting the water from the spring" method until our minivan was grounded with an expensive windshield repair. This was more than a loss of transportation for us. We relied on the van to supply us with water from the spring! Now, with no way to immediately make the repair needed, our water supply was cut off... Again!

Another great thing about our off-grid experience is that we live in a private area, out in the country past the outskirts of town, where we have neighbors but are also immersed in nature. For instance, our home backs onto a beautiful freshwater river. We sometimes swim in the river in the summertime. However, it's not easily accessible from the back of our house, as our backyard extends to a tall cliff edge at the top of a steep bluff that drops off to the water's edge far below. It's a plentiful water supply, but not easy to reach. It involves climbing down the shortest part of the hill, avoiding the snowy and icy patches, carrying two canvas shopping bags, each one holding two one-gallon water bottles. Being river water, we did not consider it to be drinkable and used it strictly for cleaning and flushing.

When this hill became too icy to safely navigate, we went to the roadside ditch, which flows into the river, and collected water from there to flush the toilet with. It was quite an experience!

This went on for about a month, even during Christmas. You may be wondering if our neighbors were concerned. We did not advertise what we were doing, but some of our neighbors surmised that we had lost our power since our house, which was often lit up with studio lighting at all hours, had suddenly become dark. Yes, some did show concern, but we did not want to be distracted with talking to anyone about our interesting off-grid adventure while we were still in the thick of dealing with it all. So, we tried to run our noisy generator during reasonable hours to draw less attention.

On New Year's Day, we purchased our generator. This was like the dawn of a new era for us and made our lives quite a bit more liveable again as we could then access our water well, hot water heater, furnace heat, fridge and other amenities for a few hours per day.

The generator was a huge deal to us. While it did not mean independence from fossil fuels, it did mean the freedom to do almost anything from any remote locale. They're optional equipment in a lot of motorhomes and camper vans. In fact, a lot of inspiration can be taken from the way these camper nomads learn to do things on the road and applied to a home-based off-grid situation.

How Much Water?

Here's how much water we needed to stay clean, well fed and healthy:

- Water for drinking. A minimum of one gallon of purified water per person per day.

- Water for bathing. We used about two gallons each for bathing. See the Bathing chapter for details.

- Water for cooking. This depends on how much is needed. We tried not to waste any water by, for example, boiling things for a long time. Estimate one gallon a day.

- Water for washing and rinsing dishes. This can be done with two large bowls or basins, one for heated hot water and anti-bacterial dish soap and the other left cold for rinsing. Two to three gallons of water to wash a pile of dishes. Try to use only non-stick pans. Eliminate any unnecessary cleaning that uses precious water when you are carrying every drop of it into the house or have an otherwise limited supply.

- Water for toilet flushing. Eight to ten gallons per day. We're lucky that we have a standard toilet that only requires us to manually pour water in its tank to flush. Though we had to adhere to the adage "if it's yellow let it mellow, if it's brown flush it down," it was still much better than a freezing outhouse in the winter. If we had to make do with an outhouse it would have been fine, but that wasn't our case.

- Water for laundry. Three gallons to wash and rinse a few small items or one larger item. Again, realizing that life can be lived on a smaller scale makes it doable. Having to worry about washing all the laundry is overwhelming, so we would take a few loads to the coin-operated laundromat. If you think in terms of self-reliance and the significance of taking small steps to help oneself toward independence and freedom, the act of doing your own laundry by hand is quite empowering! Eventually, we were able to use our washing machine to wash our clothes, but our generator was not strong enough to power our clothes dryer. This was a big deal as it's hard to get things dry, even with limited heat and power. However, we liked hand washing the things we needed when we were not able to use our generator or chose not to because of the inconvenience, noise or expense of the generator. In those cases, we hand washed a few items at a time and hung them to dry for a few days.

- Water for hand cleaning, countertops, watering plants, pets, miscellaneous housekeeping, etc. About a gallon a day.

When we carried water from the spring, we found our water usage was about 100-110 gallons per week for two adults to do everything we needed. Once we were on generator power we used a bit more, but not much, because the generator only ran for about two hours a day, so almost everything still involved jugs of water. It was much easier to refill them in the tub than go to the spring.

If you must use raw or questionable water, make sure to boil it for at least ten minutes before consuming it. This is long enough to kill even the most stubborn of water-borne cysts. We spent an incredible amount of time heating and boiling water. To reduce the amount of steam that escapes into the house and save on fuel, turn the heat to low once it reaches a boil. This is enough to allow it to continue boiling lightly and keeps the interior of the cold house from getting soaked with condensation.

If you live near the ocean, salt water can be made pure for drinking but it's not easy or cheap as you need to put it through a desalinization process first, like boiling it through a still. We did not explore this option, but the internet is an excellent source of information on this subject.

Chapter 3
Heat

Sources and Considerations

The importance of home heating can't be overstated when living in a cold climate such as Canada or the Northern USA. It can become a life or death situation if you have no way to keep from freezing. We do not want to give anyone a false sense of security when it comes to heat, so please be sure that if you need it where you will be living in your off-grid experience, you plan carefully for it and have a second emergency heat source as well, especially if you're planning on going out into the more remote areas.

Although our old farmhouse had at least one or two wood stoves throughout most of its history since it was built in 1850, almost a hundred years before electricity was brought to the area, those reliable heat sources were removed long ago. You can imagine the excitement of folks back in the day, putting in their brand new, automatic, electricity-powered, forced-air furnace system, and getting rid of their dirty, smoky, smelly, inconvenient and sometimes dangerous wood stoves and fireplaces.

Kitchen wood stove

Most insurance companies don't like them because their temperatures fluctuate depending on what they are burning, making them unpredictable (from an insurance policy standpoint), and there is a risk of chimney fires. Many insurers don't permit them at all and many others make it too difficult to bother. However, a wood stove is almost the only way to guarantee a reliable heat source without dependency on electricity, furnace oil, gas, coal, etc. Yes, you do have to buy the wood, or gather it yourself and then cure it for a year, however, if you see this coming beforehand you have a chance to prepare.

Without power, wood stoves give you a way to keep warm, cook meals and heat water for drinking, cooking, cleaning and bathing.

Small ones can be purchased and used to heat small dwellings and mobile homes. The Tiny Home and Cottage Home movements are popular and many of those homes have wood stoves. If it's not important to you to have your off-grid home insured, then putting in a wood stove might be your best move.

Cozy/tiny/cottage home movement

Unfortunately, we did not have a wood stove for our off-grid experience, so this chapter discusses the various ways that we dealt with our need for heating.

For the first few months, from October 10th to January 1st, we had no way to run our home furnace, because we did not yet have a generator.

Never leave burning candles unattended.

We had a lot of candles we had saved up over the years, which made it possible to constantly have a few candles burning close by, wherever we were in the house. We read about ways to magnify the heat of tealights by using tin pans on the bottom and placing clay flower pots or baking sheets over them to magnify the heat. We also used candles in deep jars as hand warmers.

Candle hand warmers and hurricane lamps

Candles were a major part of this experience for us. One handy technique we discovered was to keep re-using the wax from spent candles with a bit of waxed floral thread for a wick to make new jar candles, which keep the flame contained and are much safer to use and set down on a table without concern. Open flames or toppling candlesticks can be dangerous if you're not paying constant attention to them. We also found that using a hurricane lamp works great. Tapered candlesticks are a bit awkward to deal with for our utilitarian purposes and they can be dangerous because the flame is so high and exposed. We had some tapered candlesticks and used them out of necessity, but we cut them in half so they could sit below the rim of a glass hurricane lamp, recycled glass jar or votive holder.

Ensure adequate ventilation when burning indoors.

After a few chilly weeks of this, we saw that someone was giving away a nice, 24,000 BTU propane fireplace. It was quite beautiful and unique! We picked up a few copper pipe fittings for about $5 from a local plumbing supply shop so that we could attach a regular 20lb propane tank from our BBQ to it. Then we picked up a few lengths of basic chimney pipe and aluminum tape for another $20 and fashioned a fitted tin sheet collar so that we could run the pipes through a window. The chimney slope was very low, so it was tricky to light it so that the dangerous exhaust draft went out the chimney instead of into the room, but closing the room off helped and it worked.

Ensure proper chimney exhaust draft.

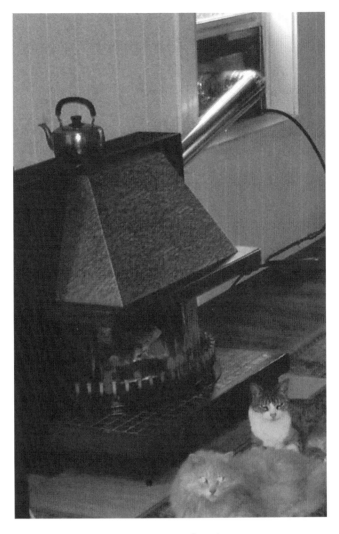

Temporary propane fireplace setup

This device performed like a real fireplace, but its heat was minimal and did not disperse through the house at all, just the five feet of space around it. As you can imagine this was not enough heat, but we had to make it enough, so we met it halfway by wearing as much clothing as possible. The two of us huddled together with our cats in front of the propane fireplace, with a few articles of damp laundry hanging nearby. The 20lb tank of propane provided about 20 hours of heat in one-hour increments. We used a bathroom scale to monitor the propane levels closely. This setup was cozy but not ideal if you have access to some other source of heat.

In a smaller home, a propane room heater like this might be just the ticket. Beware though, DO NOT run the heater with the propane tank inside your home. You need to hook it up so that somehow the propane heater is inside, but the gas tank is outside, and the chimney vents outside.

Propane is dangerous to store indoors.

If the propane tank catches fire it will act as a pressurized flamethrower and burn your house down. Another explosively deadly concern is a propane leak - the gas will pool up in the lowest part of your house (i.e. the basement) and could explode if exposed to a spark (like the furnace or water pump engaging). You know the fireball you get when you light your BBQ? Imagine that fireball a thousand times bigger in your basement! Also, the chimney exhaust fumes emitted can be dangerous and cause illness or death if you breathe too much of it and don't get to fresh air quickly enough.

Carbon monoxide is an odorless killer, so make sure you have a battery-operated CO detector mounted low to the floor; the plug-in ones don't work in a power outage.

Although at times it may seem like "Survivor: 1850s Farmhouse," you must deal with this seriously and not make any mistakes or forget.

Living off-grid can be especially dangerous because not only are you unfamiliar with doing things this way, but you often must do them in the dark, in the freezing cold, etc.

Still, compared to candle heat, we found it quite empowering to do this. High heating prices and strict insurance regulations make it hard to find freedom, but it is possible!

Since our off-grid experience, we've found new ways to deal with heating and we discovered a great item which claims to be safe for indoor use. It's called a Mr. Heater Portable Buddy Indoor-Safe Heater Box. It runs on small, disposable, 1lb propane canisters, and different models create up to 18,000 BTUs of portable heat for any room of the house. That sounds a lot easier than what we dealt with and should be enough to add some comfort to a well-ventilated room.

Mr. Heater®

Portable Buddy®

Indoor Safe Propane

Heater Box

★★★★★ 163 reviews Mr. Heater

Mr. Heater, portable, indoor propane heater

When we were off-grid and looking for something like this heater, it did not seem to exist. Now it's available at Amazon, Walmart and other camping outfitters stores. I believe that due to the growing interest in off-grid living, homesteading and the tiny house movement, heaters like these have become more available to consumers. For the low cost of $100 to $300, it's one of the more affordable answers to the problem of heating without electricity.

As always, carefully read the manufacturer's instructions for the safe operation of gas-powered appliances.

> **Burning fuel can create deadly fumes.**
> **Know what you're dealing with.**
> **Be safe.**

The New Power Generation

New Year's Day gave us a tangible reason to celebrate and marked an important milestone in our off-grid experience. We purchased our used Coleman Powermate Portable Generator.

This made it possible to run some of our appliances, including the furnace (heat!), water pump (running water!), water heater (hot showers!), fridge (cold food storage!), some extra lighting (light!) and even a small element on the stove top (hot food!). It could also power our hair dryer (dry hair!), but only for about ten seconds at a time without an overload.

An overload would mean having to wait in the dark for two to five minutes, then go outside and reset the circuit-breaker, and restart the generator (if it's ready yet). If it's winter and your hair is wet, and you don't have the heat on for more than a few hours a day, it can be uncomfortable.

Our generator was only able to run our appliances for a few hours a day and some appliances were too heavy a load to use at all, like the clothes dryer and oven. It was hard to keep our hot water heater working without serious calculation because you also need to have the water pump on, which also takes power. This was mainly because we had a limited supply of gas and many generators are quite loud, like a big lawnmower.

This is not a huge problem if you're homesteading in the woods, but for us, although we live in a rural area, there are still neighbors nearby who could hear our generator. It's not so unusual out here in the country, and those we talked to were nice about it, but optimally you might want to get a generator that is a bit quieter. These can be expensive but if you're looking to get set up off-grid and you have a higher budget, they're great. However, the point of this book is not to make you feel like you can't afford it, but to show you ways that you can.

To reduce the noise, we attached a bunch of old asphalt roofing shingles to a wood pallet frame to create a sound deadener for the exhaust pipe, which helped a little.

If you can get a strong enough generator and afford to run it, you can live and work off-grid. You'll run all your heavy power requirements, including recharging your batteries, when the generator is running, and then run lighter loads on battery power until your next generator session.

Provided we had enough gas for the generator, we had enough power to run our forced-air oil furnace, but only if we also had enough furnace oil.

In Canada's winters, the cost of home heating is not a minor bill. $1000 or more per season is a normal average for us. A further complication is the fact that all furnace oil delivery services (in our area, anyway) have a minimum delivery of $300-$500 or more.

We were short of that necessary $300 to have the oil truck come out to the house, and at the time, there was no gas station nearby that had furnace oil pumps.

Oh well, just another challenge to overcome! A bit of research revealed that furnace oil is basically the exact same fuel as the diesel they sell at the gas station pumps. The only difference is that the diesel is charged at a higher rate due to transportation and environment taxes and the furnace oil gets red dye added to it to differentiate it from the diesel. The difference in price worked out to about $1 per liter ($4/gal) for the furnace oil (which was not even an option since you have to buy in bulk) versus $1.25 per liter ($5/gal) for the diesel. That's a difference of $5 to fill a 20L (5 gal) container.

That's a bargain compared to forking out $300+ for furnace oil delivery! Plus, our local gas station gives grocery reward bucks, which pays back some of that difference.

It seems we're not alone in our thinking. Since going back on-grid, two of our local gas stations have started selling furnace oil by the liter from the pumps. You must sign a ledger stating that the oil is not intended for a vehicle.

The advantage of buying a bulk delivery is avoiding the repeated physical labor of carrying those heavy fuel containers from your vehicle through the ice and snow and then lifting them to dump their contents into your oil tank, which gets strenuous and tiresome when you have to do it every other day. Hoisting these containers high enough to pour their contents into the furnace oil drum is also hard on shoulders previously injured from pulling ripcords and transporting water bottles.

Also, by habitually walking the snowy path between the car and oil tank, that path will ice up from being packed down repeatedly and become slippery, and even on those occasional warm or rainy winter days, it will be the last to melt. So, step carefully. We have three 20L containers and tried to refuel once per week, preferably on days with nicer weather, but that wasn't always an option. It sure was a relief when we managed to save up the $300 for delivery!

All of this only applies if you need electricity for your furnace. You don't need it at all if you have a good wood stove and a reliable source of firewood. Be sure that you're only burning seasoned wood. That's chopped wood that has sat out in the elements for a year causing most of the sap and tar to rinse away. Otherwise, these gooey substances can clog up your chimney and catch fire, posing a serious risk to the safety of your home.

Woodstove and stovepipe

Unseasoned (fresh) firewood is a chimney fire hazard.

This is one of the main reasons insurance companies dislike them so much. If you don't want to chop and cure the wood yourself, you can call up a local vendor to deliver it for you, ready to burn. Don't wait until the last minute if you can help it; they are often sold out by the start of heating season, and some might even try to sell you "green" wood that hasn't cured long enough yet. If you don't know anyone to ask for a referral, look at some local houses in your neighborhood for a telltale six to eight-inch stainless steel chimney that indicates a wood stove and ask them for a firewood referral to be safe. If you have a wood stove, you should also complete annual or bi-annual chimney cleanings to prevent chimney fires.

"Going off the grid is always good for me. It's the way that I've started books and finished books and gotten myself out of deadline dooms and things."

- Neil Gaiman

Chapter 4
Transportation

How to Get Around Getting Around

Our off-grid experience changed with our circumstances. At first, we had one working vehicle, which helped us pick up water from our nearby spring, buy food and drinking water at supermarket prices and go to libraries, coffee shops and truck stops to plug in and re-juice our batteries, connect to Wi-Fi and finish our work. We also used the van to fill our propane tank for our fireplace and warm up with the van's heater which heated up nicely after a two-hour session of running the Noma Powerpack. By this time, it was usually around freezing temperatures.

This worked out well for about two months. Then suddenly, our trusty van was grounded when our hood flipped opened while driving. This ushered in a new way of doing things.

We live in a rural area, about a 15-minute drive from town. There is no public transportation system and a round trip taxi ride is $50.00 plus tip. So, even though we needed the extra $50.00, we had to cab into town for all our needs, get dropped off at one end of town, and then walk from store to store to gas station in the ice and snow to buy all our necessities, and get a cab home from the other end of town.

We were still able to use our van's engine to run our Noma Powerpack, which meant that a couple of cans of gasoline were part of our cumbersome cross-town grocery order. On the plus side, we still had a way to work and re-charge our computers' batteries. This meant we were able to continue working from home, which is a non-negotiable point for us. We would sooner give up our home and live on the road than give up our dream of being self-employed. That's how determined we are.

Through all these challenges, the freedom we came to know from starting and running our business from home kept us motivated. We were still determined - even more so than before. The freedom from having to work for someone else was more important to us than even the basic necessities which are so much harder to get while living off-grid.

Knowing that you can keep your business running while living without the electricity grid is empowering! That is why we wrote this book. We want to tell people about this new kind of freedom. Yes, it's hard, but it's possible to do this without feeling victimized.

Without the ability to go to the spring, we had to get water some other way, as we still could not access our home's well water without electricity. We looked into getting a manual pump for this, but it was prohibitively expensive.

As previously mentioned, we are fortunate enough to live next to a beautiful river at the bottom of a tall cliff. This cliff is difficult to walk down even in the summer. Still, we went down the hill with two 1gal water jugs per hand, stood on the edge of the icy river on a relatively dry rock and dipped the jugs in one by one to fill them. It would have been dangerous to fall into the fast-flowing icy water, as you can be shocked by the cold and become unable to swim.

Luckily it was okay. If you must do this, please take precautions including a buddy and a cell phone if you have one.

Always have a buddy when approaching freezing water.

If you can't afford a cellular plan, get a pay-as-you-go card voucher for $10 and save it in your wallet for emergencies. Even a phone with no minutes or SIM card has access to 911 for emergencies requiring police, fire and ambulance.

Once we carried the water back up the icy and snowy cliff and brought it into the house, how we processed it depended on how we would use it. For drinking water, we always boiled it in a teapot for ten minutes, then let it cool, and then poured it into a filtered water pitcher before drinking it. For hand washing clothes, we always used detergent and bleach to scare away any pathogens or bacteria.

Use rubber gloves while hand washing with bleach.

We used this method a few times a day until we made other arrangements. At one time it was too icy to go down to the river, so we scooped up water from the roadside ditch beside the river. This was not drinkable or good for cleaning, but it was flushable.

Keep in mind that we were both "sophisticated city folk" our entire lives, and we've each worked for well known, luxury brand companies in our previous careers, so this seems quite strange to us too, but when the cards were down, it got us through!

During this time that we had no car, we were fortunately able to walk to a nearby country general store/bakery/liquor store. They even have a propane tank exchange. Now that's a convenient store! The prices are higher than the supermarket, but when we factored in the $50 we saved on a taxi cab, we could practically go on a shopping spree there. This is also great for the local economy.

This store sells drinking water and basic food items which made it possible to buy food and water when we preferred not to pay the extra $50 for a taxi to drive us into town. With their propane tank exchange, we were also able to turn in our empty propane tank for a full one so that we could still run our small indoor fireplace to keep warm, which was still the only source of heat in our farmhouse.

We have both traveled quite a bit in the past and have a luggage pull trolley. This helped us trek to and from the store in the snow and ice with our water jugs, groceries and propane tank. Yes, it must have looked a little weird to the neighbors. A few of them made generous offers like allowing us to use their cars. But, that's not what we're here for, so we declined. Besides, what if we had smashed the windshield on their car too? Then we'd have been even further behind!

We wanted to do it all ourselves if possible, especially because we had heard of living off-grid before and wanted to try it. Of course, we could not have anticipated that we would try it by necessity.

So, with taxis to town plus our country store about a half hour walk away, we continued to be able to work from home. This continued until February. Then we found an opportunity in the local online classifieds. Someone was trying to sell their old winter beater, certified, but without any luck, since it needed some cosmetic body work and was a manual transmission. The price had dropped and dropped until it reached $250, which brought it into our affordability range... and we know how to drive stick! Hooray!

On Valentine's Day, the seller dropped off our new ride and we had freedom of mobility again! This Valentine's car, combined with our New Year's generator, gave us a wonderful sense of confidence to finish out the winter and continue our off-grid experience much more comfortably in the long run, on our own terms.

Chapter 5
Computers and the Internet

The Lifeblood of Our Business

It comes as no surprise to most that a lot of people nowadays work from home using computers. However, what is surprising is that it can be done, for the most part, without regular electricity. This is partially thanks to the power of batteries.

You know that "laptop" computers use batteries, but in our daily lives, we don't usually require the batteries to be full because our computers are almost always plugged in, right? Well, this was the key to keeping enough power on our computers to get our work done. Every minute counts with battery power so you've got to plan and be ready with charged up batteries, including spares, when your income depends on it, especially if you're like us and don't have any other forms of income coming in, such as unemployment insurance, government assistance, pension, family allowance, etc. Every dollar we spend, we work for.

So, charging the batteries in our computers was the first priority whenever we had a power session, using either the generator or the car and Powerpack inverter. But batteries don't charge quickly, so we always made sure that all our devices and battery chargers were plugged in before starting our one to two-hour power sessions each day. Of course, the power bar was only switched on after the power was flowing to protect the equipment from electrical surges, but everything was prepared in advance and ready to charge at the flick of a switch.

This allowed us to spend part of our generator session using the internet. Although we could use Wi-Fi, downloading and uploading is much faster when plugged in directly to the router with an ethernet cable, and time is so valuable in this scenario. The Powerpack would also be recharging during this time, allowing us to bank another precious hour of internet connectivity and laptop power for when the generator/car engine was shut down.

Also sold under the Duracell brand, the Noma Powerpack 1800W inverter and backup power supply unit is a super handy device that gave us the additional power we needed to run our computers and internet long enough to complete and submit our work, and pick up the next assignment.

We made sure that it was plugged in during every power session to enable us to work for longer periods of time. As this was our only source of income, it was important to turn in our work in a timely manner, with the same attention to quality. We had worked hard to establish our online business over the previous eight years before going off-grid and did not want to ruin our excellent reputation or have our valuable clients feel that anything was amiss or lacking on our end.

This was not just some fun exercise we decided to try without any worries about whether it failed. Online work is still in its infancy, and competition is fierce. We could not show any detectable change in quality that might make our clients think that we did not take their work seriously. We have not had to make a single excuse or tell a single client about our off-grid status. In fact, our business has flourished since we've been off-grid!

In the beginning, we reconfigured our studio and changed our focus on the type of work we chose to do. Previously, we were doing a lot of video production and editing, which although we were technically still able to do off-grid, it uses a lot of battery power and time spent online transferring large files, so we switched our focus to some of our other interests for which we also had regular clients, including audio recording and copywriting, which take less computer power to create, render and upload. Doing this, our business flourished the entire time off-grid, and we've been stacked with work ever since.

In our computer arsenal, we have two MacBooks and a PC laptop. We've always preferred to use laptops so that our work can be portable, as we enjoy traveling and want to be able to take our work with us.

Another way we were able to get work done when we didn't have enough battery power is to make use of the many coffee shops, libraries and truck stops in the area which have free power outlets and Wi-Fi in a heated, well-lit environment. Such luxuries!

We always budgeted a few dollars a week to buy a few coffees while we sat and worked. We always went at off-peak times so as not to annoy the staff by staying for several hours. We would choose different places each week and try not to frequent the same ones more than once every few weeks. The library is fantastic for this and your tax money pays for it, so take advantage of it if you need to or want to. The library is not just for those who can't afford to buy books. If we had to buy every book we ever read, we would never have money to spend on anything else! The sheer amount of research we do on various subjects, for both work and enjoyment, would make it ridiculous to own that many books to sit on a shelf gathering dust. The library rocks!

We used the same alternating method of visiting the local libraries. There are four libraries within a reasonably close drive from us. If we visited one, we would visit a different one the next week. No one ever bothered us at coffee shops or the library or anywhere we went, and in fact, this excuse to go out has been one of our most fun experiences going off-grid. We were able to visit and spend quality time together at libraries, coffee shops and truck stops that we would not have visited otherwise. This was something fun we did not usually do when we had all our electricity needs taken care of. Then going out for coffee or snacks every week would have seemed a bit extravagant given that we're boot-strapping entrepreneurs. But during this experience, it was like student life again and it was fun to go out into the world and be immersed in different social realms while still doing our work. This was one of the most fun things about needing to find alternative ways to do things - a guaranteed adventure was included.

For the most part, we were able to use our three laptop computers to get our work done and this included all the aspects of our work. Our social networking and interaction with the outside world suddenly became organized. We came to learn that being constantly on call to everyone was counter-productive to getting actual work done. All our correspondence could be completed within a few minutes to an hour, excluding the uploading of the larger files to our clientele that we were required to submit. This was wonderfully liberating. We have found that we don't need to be hooked up to everything that often. One to four hours of time plugged into the internet daily, preferably at two intervals of one hour each, was enough for us to get our important work information from our clients, bid on future work, check into our various business and social networks, respond quickly to emails or social posts, look up troubleshooting guides or off-grid lifestyle tips we needed to consult and even just browse a few articles for fun.

We're so thankful to our off-grid experience for opening our eyes to how much can be done with less time while staying on track. Only one of our clients likes to be responded to within minutes of his messages. We explained to him that our work sometimes requires that we are in the studio or out in the field working and we might not be able to respond to him right away, but will at some point the same day. He's happy enough with the arrangement and our service that he keeps hiring us anyway. We're thrilled to report that our work has continued, and we have been busy working ever since our original power outage.

The Smartphone

We love technology. Our smartphone is a wonderful little gadget that we use in so many ways. In our work, we do a lot of voice recording for our clients. For instance, we might create commercial ads which require a spoken script. However, printing scripts onto paper is wasteful and bringing a laptop into the recording booth would cause excess background noise in the recording. However, the smartphone allows us to have a little computer screen to use for this purpose and it does not make any extra room noise for the microphone to pick up. It uses very little power and charges in less than an hour, even when plugged into the car cigarette lighter as we drive around town running errands.

Add to that the convenience of always having a flashlight app close at hand, a calculator for keeping a close eye on our budget, fun quiz games that two people can play in the dark, easy mobile access to Wi-Fi, an emergency 911 dialler even when the pay-as-you-go card has expired and many other useful and entertaining functions. A smartphone is a wonderful device to have off-grid.

"I was born poor and without religion, under a happy sky, feeling harmony, not hostility, in nature. I began not by feeling torn, but in plenitude."

- Albert Camus

Chapter 6
Bathing

The Evolution of Our Bathing Experience

Bathing might be the biggest question on many people's minds and rightly so because it's a big deal. The difficulties of getting clean while living the off-grid lifestyle can't be overstated. We don't blame you in the least if you jumped ahead to read this chapter first! It was constantly on our minds as well, and the ways that we got and stayed clean evolved over the year that we were off-grid.

Solar Shower Bag

In the beginning, after researching a lot of this stuff on the internet, we tried a simple $10 passive solar camping shower bag. We had a lot of high hopes for solar that ultimately didn't pan out.

When our power went out, it was October 10th. Not too cold in Eastern Canada, but hardly warm either. We filled the bag with water and then laid it in the sun for as long as it was out, which was not long, especially if you factor in the clouds. The water flow from the little spout was barely a trickle, and not particularly warm. That might not be too bad if you're just using it to rinse off after swimming in the summertime, but for actual bathing, it was difficult to use. Once it gets cold outside (and inside) and your heat is limited, the thought of a cold trickle shower becomes far less appealing.

Lugging water around became a full-time chore, and the bag did come in handy as a water storage device, that is, until it ripped and became garbage. We recommend passing on this bathing option, as there are better ways.

Ice Cream Buckets

For several weeks, we were using three ice cream buckets to bathe. One for warm soapy water and two for rinsing. We needed to be careful to not melt the ice cream buckets and release toxic materials into our wash water. This method worked okay but again, bath time was a chore, not a pleasure at all.

While our well water jet pump was still working (yeah, it broke down too, sometimes when it rains it pours!), this method was not that bad. We could use the buckets with warm water to wash and then turn the shower on with cold water to rinse. It sounds harsh but it's not too bad.

If you have a strong enough generator for power and a working water pump and water heater then all you have to do is be able to afford to turn your generator on long enough to heat the water and take your showers; a two-hour interval worked well for us to get everything done. However, it does take a lot of power - more than almost anything else you do, and the generator will likely stall intermittently if it's not perfectly tuned and any other electrical device kicks in at the wrong moment. If you have a water source, a water heater and a water pump then it's no problem for you to get a good shower by having a powerful enough generator and enough gas to run often enough that you can feel clean. This is entirely possible if you're prepared with a powerful enough generator.

The Zodi Shower

We eventually found the best solution at our local big box store. It's called a Zodi Shower. It's a great little battery powered water pump that runs strong for months on just four alkaline D-cell batteries.

Reasonable water pressure from a Zodi Shower

For women especially, bathing is an important concern and strong water pressure certainly helps to get and feel clean. The Zodi delivers that and withstands hot water temperatures.

You can buy the Zodi in two ways, either just the water pump and hose ready to place into your own bucket for use, or the whole system which includes the same pump and hose plus a propane water-heating system and a pole stand. If you need these items they are probably great. However, you can use a bucket and a shower curtain for a reasonably decent shower, provided you have a water supply and a way to heat it.

The difference in price is substantial. If you want the whole system they run around $150 or so, but we were able to get the pump alone on a clearance sale down from about $35 for $25 bucks, plus another $5 for four D-cell alkaline batteries.

We already had a shower stall, a 3gal water bucket and a gas burner to heat water on, so we opted for the Zodi pump by itself.

We were so happy with this item! It won't give you a full pressure shower but it does have a reasonable amount of water pressure. For the last four months we were off-grid, we used the Zodi daily on the same set of generic batteries. Unlike all the other solutions that we came up with for showering and getting clean, this one made us feel that if we wanted to, we could live the off-grid lifestyle for a much longer period of time. If you have a supply of water and a way to heat it, you can take decent showers with the Zodi any time you want (after heating the water of course).

However, we only had a 3gal bucket of water per shower for both of us. Usually, this is how we worked that when we used the Zodi.

Shower bucket, adding cold water first to prevent melting

Do not carry boiling water, avoid accidental scalding.

First, we would heat up a 1gal pot of water on our kitchen gas stove to the boiling point (takes 20 minutes). We poured a gallon of cold water into our bucket first, then added the boiling water to make it warm without melting the bucket. Then we carried this heavy bucket upstairs to the bathroom where we had a 1gal cold water jug waiting, which we then added to adjust the temperature and increase the volume of water in the shower bucket. Then we dropped the Zodi pump into it and used the water in short bursts to rinse, soap, scrub and rinse. You can maximize the water with a washcloth and sponge.

To make it last, the water must be used in short bursts, from five seconds to a minute at most. Every drop of water must be put to work when you only have three gallons. That's about three minutes of running water. Keep an extra jug of cold water handy in case the bucket runs low and you still need to rinse.

Scrubby sponge and washcloth

It's not the spa treatment that we're used to getting with daily hot showers, however, it is possible to get genuinely clean this way. It reduced our reliance on the household electric water heater and pump, which was a real game changer.

How to Take a Cold Shower

Despite our best attempts to provide daily hot showers for ourselves, there were many times that taking a cold shower was either necessary or convenient. This occurred mainly when we had only enough generator time to shower without letting the hot water tank heat up first, or the tank did not heat up long enough for two hot showers.

This happened often enough that we discovered a technique that made ice cold showers bearable, and lucky you, we're going to share that valuable life lesson here, and save you the suffering of doing it the wrong way.

The technique is simple, and needless to say, it's best done quickly. Please consider your own health and shock tolerance. This technique is not for everybody.

First, get the cold water flowing before you step into the shower to avoid the unnecessary distraction of fiddling around with the knobs as the ice-cold water hits you. Then, aim the shower at the floor of the tub.

Here's the trick. One of the warmest parts of your body is your privates, so step in and get the water on there as quickly as you can. Don't waste time getting your feet wet, it only prolongs the pain. And don't let the water splash you above the belt line, because it's shocking when it does. You'll be surprised that the lower area endures it pretty well, if not exactly comfortably, so go ahead and get soaped up and wash your lower half. Your upper body will get splashed a little but try to keep it to a minimum. You'll instinctively try to avoid it anyway.

Here's the next part of the trick. Once you've showered your lower half, take a step back and lean your head down into the water flow and shampoo your hair and wash your face. It's more numbing than painful. Again, try to keep your upper body from getting splashed. That's still excruciating! But a funny thing happens in the short amount of time that it takes to wash your head (maybe because the brain is fooled by the cold water hitting it). Suddenly the cold water hurts less when it hits your upper body.

Take advantage of this phenomenon and adjust the shower head so that you can get fully into the water flow, upper body and all, and finish what you started. Even still, you won't need to be reminded to move quickly. Brrrr!

The next thing you know, you're done with your shower and are ready to jump out and towel off. Once you're out, the body shakes off the cold pretty quickly and you'll feel invigorated and empowered to join what must be a limited percentage of the population to undergo such an act of bravery, but most importantly, you got a shower! Way to go!

So, there it is, the tolerable cold shower formula: lower half first, head second, upper body last. Someday, you might be grateful to know it.

Other Ways to Get Clean

Soap Bottles

Throughout the course of a day, most of us brush our teeth a few times. This is another gross and frustrating thing to deal with when you don't have a lot of water on hand.

First, we used leftover dish soap bottles filled with water. This is a fantastic way to get the excess toothpaste off your toothbrush.

Water filled dish detergent bottles

Pressure Sprayer

The best method we found is to use a plant type pressure sprayer. Pump it up, then squeeze the trigger for a fine mist. These plastic sprayer bottles are great for the pressure and wonderful to mist your face, body and hair, but they can't use hot water. We use the pressure sprayer to rinse off our toothbrushes and wash our faces with an easy rinse cleansing foam. A washcloth in unnecessary for this, which is good, because they're hard to dry when you don't have easy access to a clothes dryer. Consequently, we try to use washcloths and towels sparingly.

This sprayer method works well for everyday facial and teeth cleaning rituals.

Pressure sprayer

Disposable Wipes

Another good solution for this is disposable, facial exfoliating cleansing cloths. Every day or two I use one of these to exfoliate what I would have normally removed with daily washcloth washing. These types of exfoliating cleansing wipes can be bought at the dollar stores for around $2, but if your budget allows, there are higher end ones that can cost around $15. We opted for the dollar store choice.

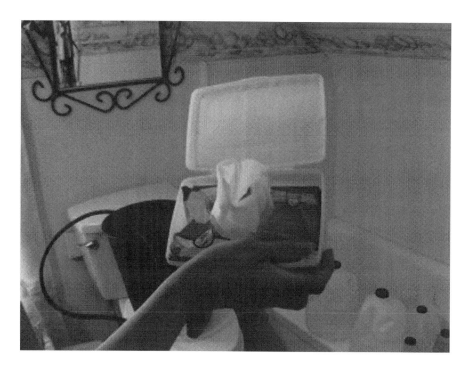

Disposable wipes

We also discovered other kinds of pre-moistened cleansing cloths that were essential in creating a more pleasant and clean off-grid experience. Here are some types of cleansing wipes:

- Flushable pre-moistened wipes. It can't be overstated how much these help both females and males to feel cleaner. Note that these are not baby wipes. These are larger, usually have a fresher scent and are indicated on the package as being sewer and septic safe, so you can flush them when you're done.

- Facial cleansing cloths (the kind which remove makeup including mascara, facial dirt and oils). These can also be purchased at the dollar store. One of the great things about these is that they usually say, "no water needed." I use one of these to wash my face and then rinse with a spritz of cool water from my pressure sprayer.

- Facial exfoliating pre-moistened cloths (as mentioned above). They are great for taking care of areas of the face which require extra exfoliation daily, weekly or whenever you feel you need it.

Hydrogen Peroxide

This handy, inexpensive disinfectant is readily available at most grocery stores, pharmacies and even dollar stores. When used with a tissue to freshen up, it can help make you feel wonderfully clean.

Hydrogen peroxide

More Off-Grid Bathing Tips

- Avoid highly lathering soaps. You must use a lot more water to remove the suds.

- All-in-one shampoo and conditioner makes it easier to wash your hair with less water.

- Short hair dries faster than long.

- Instead of using a moisturizing hair conditioner that is difficult to rinse, try using a moisturizing shampoo and then applying a leave-in conditioner after your shower. This saves a lot of water.

- Wash your hair separately. If you have long hair or hair that needs special care, wash it separately from when you take your shower. I was able to wash my hair every two or three days using three small containers. One had warm water with shampoo already dissolved in it. The diluted shampoo cleans your hair and then seems to evaporate, allowing easy use of a conditioner without rinsing the shampoo first.

- Drying your hair. Well... this is the one thing that we never found a good off-grid solution for. A hair dryer will cause a gas generator to stall if turned on for more than a ten-second hot burst, and maybe less than that. Try using the cold burst button on the hair dryer to cycle hot and cold air in ten-second intervals. The cold air uses less power.

- When you're shaving, get a small water cup to rinse your blade between strokes. It uses far less water than trying to rinse your blade under a running stream. When you're done, slowly pour off the water and all the trimmings will settle to the bottom and are easily wiped out with a piece of tissue and thrown away. If you have a battery-operated razor, then you don't need to worry about this.

Laundry

Washing clothes is another important issue you will face. When we had our vehicle in working order, we were able to visit the (not very) local laundromat. This was okay, but a bit expensive and inconvenient when you're used to doing your own laundry at home. However, it is a valid alternative, especially for drying.

The difficulty of drying laundry made it nearly impossible to wash our clothes, and more importantly, our towels and washcloths, at home. We hand washed most of our clothes and tried to hang the clothes and towels around the house and above the propane fireplace we were using to heat the living room. This method helped to get the clothes dry some of the time but usually, it was almost impossible and even resulted in a few heat-singed articles.

When we were able to use a gas generator for a couple of hours a day, we could use either a hair dryer in short bursts or hang the wet clothes over the furnace vents, but it wasn't powerful enough to run the clothes dryer. The best method requires you to wait three days until the loosely hung clothes are dry enough to wear.

It's also imperative that when you hand wash your clothes you first wrap and wring them into a towel to remove as much of the excess moisture as possible, which adds to the wet towel problem, but at least permits your clothes to dry by the time you need them.

The Stink Pile

As the wet towels and washcloths accumulated without drying, there became a need for a "stink pile." Yes, it's funny, but it smells, and not so fresh odors around the home can be discouraging at a time when it's important to remain encouraged. It's like the opposite of aromatherapy, ha!

Once we gathered a few of these stinkies, we put them in a plastic washtub, added in a little bleach and clothing soap, and then let them sit for a day or so, or until wash day. Bleach is a huge help when trying to remove the mildew and the smell that comes with it and it gives off a much more encouraging fragrance.

When we repaired our vehicle, we decided that it was well worth it to visit the laundromat. There may be better ways to dry laundry if you live in a warmer climate. We have a hanging clothesline in our yard, and while we did use this for drying some items in the summer months, it was not as reliable as we had hoped. Living in a northeastern climate our sunlight was limited, with frequent rain showers, and cold most of the year.

Our mid-size generator was not strong enough to run our clothes dryer, but you can buy a generator that can run everything if you have a couple thousand dollars to spend.

Chapter 7
Cooking

...Without a Microwave!

Like most other things about going off-grid, cooking usually takes longer than we're used to. Modern conveniences like ovens, four burner stoves, microwaves and even the good old crock pot are useless when you have no way to power them. Again, if you buy a more expensive generator, then you can probably run everything as normal if you can afford the few thousand dollars it costs plus the fuel it takes to run it. It's not cost-effective or environmentally friendly as they're all reliant on fossil fuels, but it's still a valid way to live off-grid.

At the beginning of our off-grid experience, we used our tried and true Coleman propane camping burner. It's a simple burner that screws directly on top of a disposable 1lb propane canister. We had used it before through many a power outage and it's great. The propane cylinders cost about $7 each and last about five days with normal usage for all our water heating and food prep needs.

1lb propane canisters, lasted six to seven days each

Supply adequate ventilation when cooking indoors.

Ideally, these should be used outdoors, but we used ours indoors with a window cracked open, both for fresh air to feed the flame and to help with exhaust fumes. It can be dangerous due to the inhalation of carbon monoxide fumes that might be present if there is not enough fresh air available to feed the flame and a vent to exhaust the fumes. We do not recommend that you do this, but it's what we did. We always kept the window vented open while cooking, even in the coldest months of Canadian winter, and tried to breathe fresh air as much as possible while cooking.

The Coleman Burner

With our Coleman burner, we were able to cook all our food and heat our water for nine months of our off-grid experience. This was hard for us as, even though the Coleman burner is great, it sits on top of the propane cylinder like a tower, so there's a concern that it could fall off and potentially cause an injury or fire. The gas also hisses noisily when in use, which is additionally disconcerting. I would not recommend this for going off-grid if you have kids or large pets around. Since we did not look into any other options until later, our cooking experience was a lot scarier than it needed to be.

We eventually bought extra propane to power our outdoor barbecue. This is fabulous if you can do it. BBQ cooking is delicious and easily doable in summer, or even in the snow in winter. The drawback is that someone must go out into the cold to cook it. This may not be a bad thing for you if you are outdoorsy, and we did enjoy barbecuing more often.

The Preferred Solution - Butane

Eventually we bought a single burner butane gas stove. This little wonder sits flat on the surface of your counter or tabletop. Many restaurants use these at the customer's table. This eliminated the ongoing fear that whatever we were cooking on top of the

Coleman burner would tip off. Once we got this little burner, our off-grid experience felt a lot less dangerous. These stoves are super easy to work with. The 1/2lb canister of butane locks in and out of a side compartment and a built-in clicker lights the flame automatically. The flame is quiet and hot, even compared to the propane burner. It even shaved a couple of minutes off the time it takes to boil a pot of water. Even though you still must use them in well-ventilated areas, it did not feel as weird cooking indoors with this little helper.

Our butane stove and propane oven

The Coleman Oven

One of the things we missed about having full electricity in our home was the ability to use our oven to cook. We love to bake and cook and ovens are so convenient. You can throw together some food, pop it in, run around your home or apartment for a while and Bing! It's done for you. So, once we got a little more money we bought a Coleman Propane Portable Oven on sale for about $80 (regular price $110). This runs on the same 1lb propane canisters as the first stove we had, the Coleman single burner. It's a fantastic item, large enough to cook a small chicken and a few potatoes, a frozen pizza, etc. It's capable of cooking about the same amount of food as a regular sized toaster oven, however, its footprint is a bit larger on the countertop. It's about as big as a regular sized microwave oven.

This little oven is wonderful and cooks a great chicken but it requires a little babysitting. It's not recommended that you stray too far from it while it's cooking, because even though its temperature tends to stay nice and even, sometimes it doesn't. We bought this item when we were not sure whether we were going to continue our off-grid experience and we loved it.

All in all, we have used four ways of cooking food and heating water for bathing and cleaning. In order of preference, they are:

1. The butane single burner countertop stove

2. The barbecue (a large outdoor one we had prior to going off-grid)

3. The Coleman propane portable oven (small but legitimate oven)

4. The Coleman propane camping burner

Coffee!

Without electricity, we had to find some new ways to do the same old things, including coffee-making. We begin by using our trusty stainless-steel tea kettle to boil some water on our stove burner. We used a manual Starbucks cup-at-a time plastic drip cone that sits on top of a mug. We used standard cone style paper coffee filters. We placed the coffee into the cone filter and then the boiling water went into that.

This method requires a little babysitting as you slowly pour the hot water and wait for it to drip, making sure that no coffee grounds float over the top of the filter or overflow the mug. Once again, this is not automatic. Automatic is gone.

Breakfast

We thought that keeping eggs in our daily diet was important for nutrition, especially when we were stretching every dollar and eating more instant rice and noodle dinners than usual. Cooking omelets with cheese was an easy way to cook and have less to clean. During our experience water was scarce at times, so we developed a new perspective to determine exactly how much value each item had for us, given such factors as how much time and fuel it took to cook the item and how much time and water it would take to clean everything such as pans, knives, cutting boards and graters. Even buying the ready to pour cartons of egg mixture was great because you don't need to dirty a bowl to mix it, and you won't need to rinse the goo off your hands after cracking eggshells manually. Off-grid, keeping things clean and hygienic with minimal water use is a big challenge, especially if, like us, your water supply becomes compromised.

Things like bacon or other breakfast meats are a bit harder to deal with because you will have to clean a greasy pan afterward with just a little cold water. Eliminate the things that make the most mess and change the way you do things to get the most out of the off-grid kitchen.

If you like cereals, that's great! You can have any cereal you like. We highly recommend quick oats, because unless you have a working fridge, you won't be able to keep any milk cold. This brings us to another challenging aspect of managing an off-grid kitchen...

Refrigeration

If you have a small cooler, that's great. Still, you'll need access to ice or snow at least every two to three days. We did not have a cooler, but rather stored everything in the top freezer compartment of our fridge, with a bag of ice sitting in a clean basin on the top shelf, and a newsprint liner on the bottom to absorb excess moisture from condensation.

Since we were running our fridge a couple of hours a day with our small generator, we did not buy a propane-powered fridge, although that would have been an efficient option. If you can afford to do this, you won't have to worry about refrigeration. They are not cheap, but can sometimes be picked up at a fraction of the cost from someone who is selling off the parts from an old camper trailer.

Keep food refrigerated to avoid food poisoning.

We used a mix of methods, all of which came together to give us food which was fresh enough for our consumption. Of course, buying dried goods is great if you have access to enough water and fuel to cook them. For instance, we often cooked homemade mashed potatoes the same way we did when we had electricity. When we didn't, however, peeling, cutting, boiling, mashing and washing all the utensils, cutting boards and pots involved was a lot more expensive. We don't usually advocate eating a lot of processed foods, so this was a compromise for us, but we bought instant rice and instant mashed potatoes, which require only a little water and cook super fast. All in all, these were great for being off-grid but since we're health conscious we never ate them more than a few times per week.

Eating canned foods can be a good choice, but again, only moderately. Also, they are unexpectedly messy. Our local recycling program requires us to rinse tin cans before recycling them, which takes more water. We try to eat healthily and eat as many fresh vegetables, fruits, eggs and meats as we can. The following points are useful to keep in mind:

- Buy frozen items whenever possible. It equals free ice! Try this especially for meats. You can get some veggies this way as well but they can get soggy in the bag. Buy your meats pre-cut or boneless if possible for less mess and waste later.

- Expect your perishables to only last around four days. The meats will defrost in a day or two even with ice and other frozen products.

- You can choose to buy a whole cabbage or chopped cabbage like coleslaw mix. Any way you can get it, get it. Cabbage lasts a long time, is a cost-effective superfood and your health will benefit from even just adding it to salad. It's still cost-effective to buy it already shredded so we say go ahead. Pre-washed salad is value added! No water needed! If you can wash things easily and can shred your own, by all means, buy the whole cabbage. If your budget can afford it, you can choose to buy pre-cut and washed vegetables. Since keeping things clean is a huge priority now, it's worth it if you can afford to have all the processing done for you. This is great for folks trying to live out of a camper van, for instance. Water is always a challenge for them. Buying the ready bagged salad is recommended if you can afford it. Eating salad every day is important for maintaining your health; there are no sick days off-grid and it's a lot of work!

- Nut and seed mixes are awesome both for their quick snack ability and their health benefits. So are non-hydrogenated nut butters, but those aren't as easy to clean as the nuts themselves.

- We love to bake our own bread and make our own cookies, but we found that given all the effort it takes to mix, bake and clean afterward, we got a lot of value out of buying the store-bought items. For us, this is a big deal because we always try to live cost-effectively and buying pre-made items is not as healthy or inexpensive. However, when we factored in all the effort it takes, we decided to indulge in some of these items. We splurged on bread, rolls, cakes, pies, cookies, gluten-free items, flatbreads, naan bread and tortillas, cheesecakes, breakfast rolls, cinnamon sticky buns, muffins and the best one of all, bakery birthday cakes! Don't get the idea that we went cake crazy; if you take inventory of what you buy in a year, you probably buy a lot of the above items. Indulging in these pre-made, store-bought goodies was one of the unexpected perks of going off-grid.

- Buy a whole pre-cooked chicken, ham, meatloaf, etc. and plan to consume it the day you bring it home and/or the next day if you have sufficient refrigeration. You will only have to reheat it, not cook it for 45 minutes, saving your valuable fuel.

- Eggs don't need much refrigeration, so they are an excellent choice for going off-grid. Some vegetables and most fruits don't need refrigeration. Pay attention to how they are displayed in the grocery store to determine if refrigeration is necessary; they are experts at stretching the freshness of produce and making it last.

- If you want fresh meats, buy small amounts of boneless meat that is pre-cut for quick cooking. We often ate higher quality cuts of meat than usual by doing this.

- Pasta takes too long to cook. Even good ol' mac & cheese takes ten minutes and that's too long sometimes - not to mention a waste of cooking water that gets poured down the sink. Go for ramen noodles as a side dish instead. It's not as nutritious as some, but you'll find when living off-grid that fast becomes very important. Go with Chef Boyardee and a salad for a quick, easy meal. Without a microwave food prep will take more time, but it can be fun.

- Milk, cheese and dairy items become a problem to store for long, but if you buy a small amount you should be able to keep it cool for a day or two. If you need cream for coffee you can use the powdered kind. Of course, watch out for hydrogenated oils. You don't want to neglect your nutrition and health.

Ideas for Off-Grid Meals

Breakfast

- Two eggs omelet with cheese and veggies. Tip: Use frozen spinach as a block of ice for refrigeration, then when it turns soggy cook it into beautiful Eggs Florentine by adding it to your omelet. Scrambled eggs tend to stick to the pan and are tougher to clean, so go with the omelet instead.

- Eggs with fried potatoes and fresh fruit, such as a sliced apple. Eggs are a great source of nutrients - we try to eat them almost every day.

- Quick oats with a bit of peanut butter and sugar or sweetener. We became good friends with oatmeal, even for dessert. It's so good for you.

- Plain or flavored regular or sugar-free yogurt. The individual, recyclable containers are useful and perfect for adding a few sunflower seeds. The larger container is too hard to keep fresh. In this case, smaller is better.

Lunch

- Tuna on salad with seeds, cheese and a slice of bread. Choose whole grain bread for extra nutrition and flavor, like 100% whole wheat, ancient grains, flax, oat, etc. There are many delicious varieties to choose from.

- Store-bought soup or chili with a salad and bread or crackers. Deli is best, but canned is fine and usually more affordable. If you can buy it frozen that's best, as it will be more nutritious than canned and have the added value of providing extra refrigeration for your cooler. Cook it after it thaws on its own; there's no need to waste valuable fuel by melting valuable ice.

- Deli-style sandwich of your choice with lettuce leaves or sprouts.

- Ramen with added vegetables. Try whisking a whole egg into the boiling soup with a bit of soy sauce to give it that feeling of Asian style egg-drop soup. Look at you, living in an off-grid gourmet kitchen!

Dinner

- Barbecued fish with zucchini and cheese-filled peppers (all cooked on the BBQ). Buy fish which is already cleaned and de-boned, otherwise there's too much cleanup. Barbecued fish tastes amazing!

- Pan-cooked breaded boneless chicken thighs or breasts. Use quick oats instead of breadcrumbs or whole grain flour for a healthier, heartier coating. Serve quick cook rice or instant potatoes and a big, happy salad with this one. Make sure your salad has shredded cabbage or carrots for extra nutrients.

- Any pre-cooked sausage such as cheddar smokies or kielbasa chopped and stir-fried with some onions and any other vegetables you like that can cook quickly. If you like kale, that's great! If not, maybe you should give it another try. It's super healthy and won't melt away like spinach. You can rip it up and put it into the pan with the cooking sausage, no knife or board needed to clean.

- Canned pasta dinner like Chef Boyardee. There's as much food in that big can as a $10 store-bought lasagna and it will be ready in… oh, it's already ready! You just warm it and serve. You will want to be able to cook a fast dinner sometimes, so it's great to have these in the pantry. You'll come to appreciate the small victories and advantages it affords. Always serve with a salad or even some coleslaw.

Snacks and Drinks

- We always try to have easy to eat fruit such as bananas on hand. We also buy big bags of apples so that some fresh fruit is always available. Fruit that requires minimal peeling and cutting is your friend.

- Popcorn, when made at home on a stove top (not microwave popcorn), is inexpensive, almost a health food and is easy to make off-grid. Make a double batch while you're at it and put some in sealed containers for easy snacking throughout the week.

- Ready-made cookies, bread, mixed nuts or anything you want and can afford. However, the perishables go fast if you don't have refrigeration.

- We love herbal tea and even instant coffee so our kettle takes care of most of our beverage needs for us. Occasionally, we order take-out when we're able to get into town, especially fried chicken (chicken takes so long to cook!). That's when we indulge in something like a fast food meal with a soft drink. Rarely do we drink sugary drinks - even juice unless it's homemade.

- Skip it! Sometimes the difficulty of having to cook a meal made us say, let's skip it. Pre-made popcorn with fresh fruit for dinner is filling, delicious, healthy and as easy to clean as it is to prepare. Plan in advance and have a few quick wins for those days when you're not up to the challenge of cooking and cleaning up after a full course meal.

"Most of the luxuries and many of the so-called comforts of life are not only not indispensable, but positive hindrances to the elevation of mankind."

- Henry David Thoreau

Chapter 8
Cleaning

How It's Different

Living the off-grid lifestyle, one quickly discovers that getting clean is harder than staying clean. That may sound like an enigmatic sentence. Once off-grid you will understand.

The luxury of running water is difficult to do without, even with abundant natural water supplies nearby. Although our old farmhouse is next to a fresh river, it was a challenge to get enough water.

Keeping things clean in such a way that you FEEL comfortable is a huge battle won in enjoying your self-sufficient lifestyle, rather than feeling victimized by the circumstances.

Cleaning Needs:

- Personal (see Bathing chapter)
- Laundry
- Dishes, pots, pans and utensils
- Home and surroundings

Doing the Dishes

Since when you're off-grid you most likely won't have a working dishwasher, it's important to rinse or brush off the dirty dishes without letting them sit out too much. Since our water was limited we had to let some dishes pile up for a few days until we had enough water to wash them by hand. This is how we arranged our dish-washing:

- We heated up a gallon of water in one of our large pots on our butane stove.

- We then placed about a half of a gallon of cold water into a washing bowl/tub. We used a big plastic one. It's important to put the cold water in first so that you don't melt your wash container. When the water is hot, add some to the cold water until it's full enough for most of your dishes to be mostly submerged.

- We use Palmolive antibacterial dish soap for most things. Antibacterial because it's good to have that little extra assurance that you're clean, and Palmolive because it's the one that is "soft on hands." This makes a big difference when you're using it a lot. Also, try to use only the kinds without added lotions. Water is a precious commodity and not just water, but water pressure is a huge factor in trying to get extra soap or lotion off your hands or body. The less water needed to use and wash the product off, the better.

- Now we have our first washing container with warm water. Next, we use a large container with cold water for rinsing. If you like, you can heat up more hot water for your rinsing purposes, but we found that cold rinse water was fine.

- It takes a while to learn the small ways that you can be your own best friend by changing the way you do things. For instance, if you can eliminate any of the stuck-on gunk beforehand that you would otherwise have to spend time scrubbing, that's going to help you get through it faster, while your water is still warm. If you have anything with residue in it, use a little of your warm soapy water on the item first. However, only do one or two at once and then re-use that water to soak other dishes. Yes, it's yucky but it works. Water is such a precious commodity we have no idea how much we overuse it daily. Try to only use a small amount of soap as it can eat up your water quickly and make it harder to rinse.

- We started with the least soiled dishes, which were usually glasses, then cups and mugs, followed by bowls and plates, followed by utensils and finally pots and pans. Most of the gunk settles to the bottom. Don't traumatize yourself by looking in the water past the suds. Instead, be amazed at how clean your dishes are!

- It took us about four gallons of water to do a whole load of dishes. We were only able to get around to doing our dishes every few days, so our water use for dishes looked something like this:
  - One or two gallons of water for washing
  - One or two gallons of water for rinsing

- Leave the dishes on a drying rack to drip dry before you towel dry/polish them and put them away, otherwise you'll have to deal with another wet towel.

- As far as disinfecting goes, our usual Comet-style scrub cleanser is not appropriate for off-grid use as it requires a lot of water to remove. We use a spray bottle with generic lemon-scented disinfectant and then wipe down with a paper towel and water. We keep a second bottle of 10% bleach and water solution for sanitizing the counters and sink after they've been cleaned, and the kitchen smells great.

Hooray for another victory!

Laundry

As you might imagine, our washer and dryer are not able to run without electricity. Our laundry journey has taken many roads. First, we hand washed most items and then tried hang-drying them. This was pretty good but some of our clothes were too big to hand wash and would not dry hanging in the house, even for days. We used the coin-op laundromat when we were able to, but for the four months that we were stuck without a car, it was up to us to figure it out.

Here is an important fact about going off-grid that deserves to be repeated: Most things take longer than you are used to. Like, much, much longer. We gained a new respect for the way people must have lived in the days before electricity on demand. Because we have the advantage of working for ourselves from home we had the time to do those extra chores. We were more active and we both lost weight.

Again, I stress that finding new ways to do things is helpful. When we had our generator running we could use our washing machine, but our generator was not powerful enough to run the clothes dryer, which is the harder chore to accomplish when you live in a cold climate. Also, we ran a clothesline outside in the summer, but that was not enough either, as not every summer day is a sunny one. At one point we were holding the wet clothes up in front of the propane fireplace. This worked a little, but it was time-consuming, and some items never seemed to get completely dry.

We ultimately found that wearing two or more sets of clothes at once, by dressing in layers, was a good idea. We usually wore underclothes like leggings or long johns, tank tops and T-shirts with long-sleeved shirts and heavy sweaters in the colder months. This way our outer clothes, which tended to be heavier and harder to wash and dry, would need less frequent washing and drying. The lighter underclothes were smaller and easier to hand wash/dry more frequently.

Also, when our generator and furnace were running we could hang our clothes above a heat register and this helped quite a bit. However, this was difficult, as we couldn't run the generator and furnace all day long, just a couple of hours a day. If you live in a warm climate this might not be as much of a problem for you, but it is challenging when it's cold.

It was hardest to keep things like kitchen towels, bath towels and washcloths from attracting mildew. Our answer to this was the "stink pile." We put them together in a washtub with bleach for at least a few hours before attempting to wash them. This way we were free of the nasty odor, and that's quite liberating.

As with most things off-grid, if you have an alternate way to power appliances at least some of the time, such as a generator, this won't be a problem for you.

House Cleaning

Without a vacuum cleaner, we found that sweeping the carpeted area a few times with a clean broom was enough to remove much of the visible dirt. We like to spray a fabric refresher spray afterward, as it deodorizes and helps to cut down on dust as well.

We also found a wonderful little item called a Bissel Sweep-Up. It's one of those old push-style movie theater carpet sweeper things. We paid only $15 for it on sale. They sell for $40 or so.

Cleaning Floors

Without much water, cleaning floors becomes tricky. The best way to do this with as little water as possible is to use a spray bottle with your chosen floor cleaner diluted in water. Spray the specific areas you need to clean and wipe with a sponge or a paper towel. Skip the mop altogether, as it takes too much water use. We try to limit our use of paper towels but when you're off-grid they can be a big help. Old newsprint sales fliers are also very absorbent and useful for cleaning up floors that are wet from dripping boots and other wet and dirty messes.

Cleaning Sinks and Showers

Sometimes it's best to use a good bleaching cleanser like Comet to clean the toilet, shower and sinks as usual. This takes a few gallons of water to properly rinse out all the dirt, soap buildup, etc.

Additionally, spritzing the shower from time to time between cleaning with a bleach solution kept it from becoming too musty. Our handy dandy manual pressure washer spray bottle was great for this. We used it to spray off the bleach solution.

Cleaning the Loo

There's no way around it, the toilet will be dirtier if you are not able to flush it as often. If you have an outhouse or some other arrangement, this won't be such a problem for you. Even if you have a portable toilet like some of the noble folks living out of their vans and motorhomes, you don't have to let waste sit in the toilet. Keep air freshener, scented candles and incense in the bathroom. Aromatherapy is any off-gridder's friend!

Each time we flushed our toilet, it took two gallons of water. This meant we had to obtain, bring home and carry two gallons of water upstairs for each flush. We kept several gallons of it in the bathtub and carefully monitored the water to flush ratio budget.

When we got our generator and could run on limited power, we were able to run the water pump to refill our jugs right there in the tub for later use. No more water weight-lifting from the van and up the stairs! However, we could only run our generator a couple of hours a day, so we still had to limit our water use between refills.

During generator time, we could also take cold showers, and sometimes hot showers, but our time was always limited. We often used this generator time to run around the house and do all the chores and check the internet to keep our business going. The generator is loud, so we tried to run it at hours that were not too bothersome for our neighbors. Like most things, if you can afford a $2,000 silent generator then you can have a pretty nice experience!

Chapter 9
Batteries and Gadgets

Convenient Off-Grid Helpers

Batteries were such a huge part of our off-grid experience that we felt they deserved a chapter of their own, but equally important are the devices that they power, so here we'll share our experiences with gadgets.

We used a wide variety of batteries throughout our experience, some rechargeable and some disposable. We had rechargeable batteries in the computers, smartphone and Noma Powerpack that we discussed in previous chapters.

We also have several sets of AA rechargeable batteries and a charger that can charge two at a time in about an hour. We always made sure we had this charger loaded and plugged in any time we ran power to the house, either by generator or car engine/Powerpack. We also made sure to bring it with us any time we visited a coffee shop or library to get some work done. These AA batteries worked hard to power our flashlights mainly, but also to power our digital camera, a small radio, keep the household clocks ticking, etc.

The dollar store is by far the best source of cheap batteries. Usually, for a dollar or two, you can get a package of batteries in whatever size you need - even rechargeables.

We also got a handy flashlight/lantern combo there that improved our experience. Prior to that, we had a couple of hand crank flashlights that don't require batteries, but they do require near constant cranking, and neither was designed to stand on its own, requiring one hand to hold it at all times and another to crank it. They were impractical to use while trying to cook or get almost anything else done that might require a free hand or two. The cranks on both died fairly quickly, even after a repair attempt, requiring an upgrade to the AA battery-operated LED flashlight/lantern we purchased for $3.

In addition, we also had a AAA battery-operated LED headlamp that we had bought previously for $2. These are miner-style lamps that strap to your forehead and illuminate whatever you are looking at. It is often necessary to have the use of your hands while doing things in the dark, whether cooking or repairing a generator. Two of those headlamps died, but they are so affordable we replaced them with another, and it is still working. We were also able to combine the parts of the two dead ones to repair one of them, so now we have two working headlamps. The $3 lantern/ flashlight is still working great and has never needed repair. We'll talk more about this one shortly.

The AAA batteries we used are the cheapest disposable zinc oxide ones we could find, five for $1.25 at the dollar store. Our AA charger will fit AAA batteries, but we were never able to find a set of rechargeable AAA batteries that were affordable, at least not while we were still off-grid. Recently we visited a new Ikea store in our area and they had the best deal we've seen so far on AAA rechargeables, and Amazon also has some pretty good deals if you can afford a larger quantity package and the shipping costs. For us, $1.25 every couple of months was too good to beat.

Another surprisingly useful item is the little LED tea light candles. They run on two or three watch batteries, and their plastic flame flickers with a realistic, golden candlelight. We got ours in a six pack, and when all six are lit, the living room feels warm and cozy. They're like candles that you can place anywhere without causing a fire, so it's okay to put them in the fancy dishes, or on the photo shelf, the Christmas tree or corners and niches where you would not put an exposed flame. We've run ours for probably over a hundred hours so far, with nightly use over several weeks, and still haven't had to replace the batteries. Real tea lights have the advantage of creating heat, which is nice if you put them in a ceramic wax or oil burner or other warming container. However, the safety advantage that LED tea lights have over actual tealight candles easily justifies the small expense.

To break the comparative costs down, the best deal on tea light candles is 20 for $1, each providing four hours of flame, for a total of 80 hours of light per dollar. We paid about a dollar each for the LED tea lights and got over 100 hours of light from them with no risk of a house fire, optimal lighting placement options and the convenience of not having to relight all the candles every four hours or deal with bagfuls of the little aluminum cups that are left over when the tea light candle is done. These cups are not recyclable, and we hope they're going to come in handy for some obscure purpose someday, so we're hanging on to them, even though we have no idea what that might be!

We also have a small portable radio that runs on a 9V battery, which was nice to have around the house, especially while cooking or cleaning. The sound of local music stations helps make things feel less eerie in a house with no power and makes chores more fun.

In the summer months, it gets quite hot without any air conditioning. Anytime it got too hot we could take a cold shower, but we also purchased a couple of tiny, personal battery-operated fans. These small but noisy devices can hang on a cord around your neck and blow a bit of air across your face, or if you prop them up on the bedstand they'll circulate a bit of air to help you sleep. They run on AA batteries for about an hour before dying out, so it was good to have all the batteries charged up for these hungry devices.

Additionally, we have an oscillating desk fan that runs on USB power or four AA batteries. The fan blades are about six inches across and it blows a nice stream of air while being surprisingly quiet. But again, like the smaller fans, it can burn through a set of rechargeables in about an hour, and when it's plugged into the USB of a laptop, you have to make sure it doesn't drain the laptop battery unnecessarily.

The fan motors would probably run longer on a set of alkaline batteries, but since those are disposable we kept cycling through several sets of rechargeable AA batteries. They don't last forever and eventually, they will refuse to be recharged, but our several sets of trusty 800mAh Sunbeam batteries lasted us many cycles and surely saved us money and battery waste in the long run.

Shortly after we got reconnected to the grid, we came into possession of a pair of solar lanterns. Sounds like an oxymoron, right? Well, these amazing lanterns would have made a huge impact while we were off-grid, and we still use them frequently today. Keep them in a window or quick charge them on a USB, and the ultra-bright LEDs are capable of illuminating a room (dimly), for up to 12 hours, just in time for the next solar recharging cycle. They are more expensive than a dollar store light, and run somewhere in the $20-30 range but, wow, are they fantastic! We have one with an inflatable, transparent, cylindrical, beach ball style lamp shade that's good for lighting a wider area like the living room, and another that uses a transparent water bottle for the lampshade that has a much brighter, more even light that is good for lighting a dining table, cooking area, workbench, etc. If your budget can afford one of these it will surely add to your convenient lighting, which is hard to get enough of when you're off-grid.

"It is better to risk starving to death than surrender. If you give up on your dreams, what's left?"

- Jim Carrey

Chapter 10
Lighting

Lights for Different Uses

Lighting is so important and believe us, you don't know how much you rely on it until you can't see a darned thing when you really need to. In the beginning, as we fumbled our way through learning curves of how to deal with this and that, our evolution of lighting went something like this...

For the first few weeks, we used wind-up solar flashlights for most uses. We tried to find ways to get away from the dependency on traditional ways of doing things. We already had one wind-up flashlight and we stuck to that one and a few other battery-operated flashlights that we had around the house.

However, the most helpful light we had was an LED headlamp. In our home, it's usually used for working in the basement or under the cabinets, where it's dark. We only had one to start with, so one of us used the headlamp and the other used the wind-up flashlight. This worked out surprisingly well. With an inexpensive battery-powered headlamp, a wind-up flashlight and the daylight hours, we moved through the early days of our off-grid experience. Candles were also used every day in some way, for both heat and light.

In our vocal booth, where we record audio products for clients, we used a smartphone and an LED booklight to illuminate the small work area.

Getting up earlier to get as much done as possible during daylight hours was also something we enjoyed about being off-grid. Depending on the natural light is soothing and is an easy routine to get used to.

We needed more light, so we went to the dollar store and got another LED headlamp and a small, handheld, three-way LED flashlight. This small flashlight only cost $3 and can work as a powerful flashlight, be flipped open on the side as a table lamp or closed for a soft night light. It can be stood on one end so that it will stand up beside a sink, stove, etc., while most flashlights do not seem to want to stand up at all. When bathing, shaving or trying to brush your teeth at night, you can imagine how important lighting is. This small flashlight was perfect for personal use.

Anything USB powered was awesome. We found a great plug-in USB light that used very little power and could light up an entire small room. We also bought a small phone charger/power bank, again from the dollar store, for about $4. It looks identical to the Duracell version for $25 and works great. None of our equipment in the beginning was very expensive.

Our lighting needs were best met in the following ways:

- Headlamps for all. The $2 dollar store one was great and comparable to those costing $10 or more. Once we bought one from the dollar store that didn't work at all. They exchanged it with no questions asked; they didn't even need to see the receipt. So much for expensive warranties!

- A small personal 3-in-1 flashlight for each person which can be stood up and used hands-free, from the dollar store for around $3. This was the light we used most, and still do.

- Wind-up flashlights for when there are no more batteries around or because you prefer them. They're amazing and reliable (no batteries required), but hard to use one-handed, and not extremely durable. Both of ours died after a few weeks of heavy use. They're around $15 and sometimes come with a radio and phone charger outlet - both huge pluses.

- A plug-in USB light and a spare USB power bank to run it, from the dollar store for about $3-4 each.

- Candles, but always in high glass or metal containers so that the flame is well contained. Buy as many bags of inexpensive tea lights and candles as you can find. We had drawers full of them and used every single one. To get the most out of your tea lights, only use them when you can let them burn the full four hours they're good for. If you blow them out before they are done, they won't last long at all when you relight them - the wax needs time to melt.

- The reusable LED tealights might reduce your dependency on disposables.

- We also obtained light from a standing office lamp plugged into our Noma Powerpack, so when we were on the internet we had plenty of light from that as well.

- Of course, when the generator was running, we could light the whole house normally, and we would use that time to complete as many chores as possible.

In the beginning, the lack of light while trying to do things that used to be second nature was weird. We had a few broken glasses and scrapes from bumping into things and knocking things over in the dark. Once, a candle holder fell off the medicine cabinet and cracked our porcelain sink, adding yet another expense.

Once you get over the learning curve, it seems more natural to live this way. By only using what you require, you come to appreciate natural light.

Chapter 11
Exercise

When the Treadmill Doesn't Work

Keeping fit while living as we did, off-grid, house-bound in a remote area, in the winter, is a challenge. When you don't leave your house much, especially in the snow or harsh weather, it's important to find a way to get some exercise.

At the beginning of our off-grid adventure, we still had a working car, so we were able to drive to interesting places to swim, walk, jog, etc. We don't own gym memberships but try to take a walk every few days.

We sit down at our computers so much that we forget to get up and get the blood circulating sometimes. To compensate, we adhere to a strict walking schedule whenever possible (at least every other day for 30-60 minutes, year-round).

However, when our car needed unaffordable repairs in the dead of winter we had to find another way to get that crucial exercise we so badly needed, and still work from home - other than trudging through the snow to buy groceries and fuel, that is.

The solution? A stationary bike. Our wonderful stationary bike has allowed us to jump on it for a few minutes a day to get a good workout, which, while not usually super high-intensity, does the job of getting our heart rates up and our muscles and lungs going.

It makes you feel better almost instantly, PLUS there's another off-grid advantage. When showers are difficult to come by and staying clean is so important, riding the bike slowly for a few minutes at a time gives you a bit of a workout without making you all sweaty and pungent. The importance of this can't be overstated. Seriously.

Another viable option: Get a gym membership. If you live near a gym, have a car or bus route to get to one and the money to join, a gym membership is one of the most wonderful things you can have while living off-grid. The hot showers alone are worth it! Sitting in front of a computer often can cause back, leg and hip problems, so if we could have afforded gym memberships for both of us, our experience would have been much more comfortable, as exercise (and showers) are so important.

However, we did not have this, so we mostly walked around our neighborhood and used the stationary bike daily. There is a high-intensity training method for cycling, called HIIT, pronounced "hit." This kind of workout helps to get the most out of the short, power-sprint type of cycling that was doable while we were off-grid. However, we only did this when we knew a shower was possible, because we would sweat. We also maintained almost daily routines of stretching, isolations, weight training and isometrics.

Once we got our transportation fixed, a lot of options opened up to us once again. We actually bought another car for less than it was going to cost to have our original car fixed. Living off-grid is a lot more comfortable if you have a car to break up the monotony of being at home without power for a long time, especially in winter. BUT, it was still a lot of fun when we did not have a car, even though it got pretty rugged trying to get water and do other things. Don't think that you cannot do it because you don't have a car. You can! We did.

"There is greater anxiety, commonly, to have fashionable, or at least clean and unpatched clothes, than to have a sound conscience."
— **Henry David Thoreau**

Chapter 12
Off-Grid Income

Running a Home-Based Business Off-Grid

Since 2007, we have worked from home as freelance providers of graphic design, photography, audio products, editing, writing and more. We work almost exclusively online and opportunities for those who have internet access abound in that realm.

Checking in two or three times per day allowed us to upload our completed work, communicate with clients and bid on new jobs. Then we turned the internet off (AC power) but were able to continue working on our computer batteries.

We spread our workload out over three computers - two Macs and one PC. We also have a smartphone which we use as a teleprompter for when we need to read and record a voice-over script. It's also a handy flashlight and has a few trivia games installed that two can play in the dark.

However, we do not use our cell phone for calling, texting or surfing the net. We have no cell phone plan; we keep a pay as you go card in our wallet in case of an emergency.

You can still use the phone with free Wi-Fi to get email and messages from the internet without using the actual "phone" part and it does not cost you anything if you have Wi-Fi access, whether at home or at the library, coffee shop, grocery store, mall, etc.

How to Find Work

Living off-grid doesn't mean that you have to work from home. There are always jobs of some sort in your area, no matter where you live. Day jobs, in addition to wages and regular benefits, offer conveniences such as a heated, well-lit building to spend your days in, with cafeterias, running water, toilets and sometimes even showers. You won't find those benefits listed on many job descriptions, but they are real benefits!

However, something about the off-grid lifestyle begs that we work from home, as it is truly where our heart is. Fortunately, in this new millennium, remote online jobs are plentiful, and it's what we know best.

There are a ton of online freelance marketplaces and other remote employment opportunities posted on the internet. The reality, however, is that many online work opportunities do not pay well (although some certainly do), mainly due to the enormous volume of highly talented individuals around the world already working online.

It can be difficult in western societies to compete with freelancers in some areas of the world where the average annual income is less than $1000 per year, and geography is no indicator of talent.

Even in the same town, competing freelancers can offer as low of a price as they choose if they want the job. Price isn't everything, but this factor does have the effect of lowering the overall market rates in general.

On top of that, most every website designed to help you find work is going to take a slice of your pie when you do, in the form of a commission, often in the 20% range. Being aware of this in advance helps to approach each job with a proper mindset, rather than face discouragement after the fact.

Fortunately for you, you have the advantage of no power bill, since you live off-grid! Our advice is to take the lower paying jobs from a variety of areas to stay busy and get your portfolio established, and then work your way up from there. Your niche will eventually define itself, and gradually your portfolio, client base and reputation will be enough to support you in the industries you wish to focus on. Always be working or looking for work, and you'll miss very few of the best opportunities and always have some money coming down the pipeline.

Alternatively, waiting for someone to pay you a top price without the experience to justify it is an incredible long shot. But hey, it's up to you, and a strong enough self-marketing plan for someone who is sufficiently motivated might overcome many disadvantages. Just a couple of great gigs can make your year!

Where to Look

Internet search is your friend. There's no point in listing all the amazing resources available online, as they change constantly, and what works well for some today won't tomorrow, and vice-versa. The key is to find what works for you, so prepare to spend at least twice as much time looking for work as you spend working. Finding work is by far the biggest part of our job.

Are you good with telephone work? There are all sorts of work-from-home customer service opportunities that pay reliable part-time and full-time income. Most even offer benefits with room for promotion and advancement.

One of the main reasons this is such an easy opportunity to break into is the high rate of employee turnover, or churn. The work can be psychologically stressful, as most of these telephone customer service and sales positions involve a significant amount of rejection, complaints and even hostility from irritated and impatient prospects and customers.

But if you're able to keep a cool head, this can be a quick way to make a regular paycheck from the comfort of your own quiet home office. You will need to prepare a battery backup for your system, however, as these jobs require a constant connection to the internet while you work your shift. With regular pay, you can afford to continue to pursue other job opportunities in your off time. Again, spend most of your time working and looking for more work.

Are you good at writing or making social media posts? There are endless opportunities for social media community managers and blog article writers for just about every industry you can think of. Whatever you know about and write about, there is likely someone looking for you to do that for their company. The trick is finding that opportunity, which takes a lot of internet searching, networking and perseverance.

Often you'll spend enormous amounts of time to finally land a gig, only to find that despite the promise of ongoing work, it is just a one-time job. Don't take it personally. Sometimes the employer is a risk-taking entrepreneur with the highest of hopes, but there are no guarantees when you're freelancing. With time, you will eventually build a portfolio and repeat client base and be able to dedicate more time to this revenue channel.

Are you entrepreneurial? There are many websites that will allow you sell your own handicrafts, digital products, administrative help, typing, voice over and other creative services, or you can set up a YouTube channel to post your own videos and try to build an audience, or you can offer online coaching. The possibilities are endless, but be prepared to put in years of time to build a reputation and following before you can rely solely on this type of income.

It sounds like a long time, but a year flies past like a week when you're busy doing what you love, so don't hesitate to set long-term goals, even if your present situation feels overwhelmingly demanding.

Chapter 13
Going Off-Grid for Good

Living the Dream

Because of our experience and research, we'd like to share with you our advice on how we would choose to go off-grid if we had the budget and time to prepare.

In your mind, the idea of living on your own, independent from the electricity grid, may seem far-fetched. However, people found ways to survive and thrive long before the power grid existed, and today we have many modern luxuries to make things easier.

The key is to realize that you'll be doing things differently. Having a mindset of approaching familiar tasks with different methods of accomplishing them is helpful, and practically a necessity.

Generators

The easiest way to switch over with the least amount of inconvenience is with a good, whole house, silent generator. With one of these, you'd probably hardly even notice that you're off-grid. Except, that is, for the recurring fuel bills. It won't be cheap to run that thing around the clock! They often run on natural gas or propane, sometimes gasoline, and best of all, but also rarest and most expensive, diesel.

Diesel has the advantage of allowing you to go truly off-grid, by learning how to distill your own biodiesel oil from various non-petroleum sources. There are some more affordable vintage diesel generators for sale that are still in excellent condition, but they are massive, heavy and noisy.

The newer ones are quite nice! However, gasoline, natural gas and propane all leave you reliant on a different kind of grid, the fossil fuel supply chain, and fracking gas wells. Ick! Not near my drinking water well, please!

Until you get your biodiesel algae farm up and running, furnace oil is a direct substitute for diesel (and vice versa) and is legal to use in generators. You can even have it conveniently delivered directly into an oil tank beside your house like most oil heated homes do.

To the best of our knowledge, it is the same low-sulfur diesel fuel, but furnace oil has a red dye added to it to indicate that it has not been taxed for Highway Traffic Environmental Transportation Tariffs, and it's not legal to use in diesel-powered vehicles. However, it is relatively affordable and stores easily in large quantities for long periods of time without spoiling, evaporating or exploding.

At a minimum, our small portable gasoline generator was enough for us to get through. We would not recommend that it be your only source of power for heat and water, because if it fails (and it probably will at some point), you will need an alternative. This can be solved with two generators, but you'll still have a challenging time juggling what electrical appliances you can run at all, run together, and when.

Alternatively, and perhaps even preferably, propane or natural gas both offer the huge advantage that the same fuel can also be used with a gas furnace, a gas hot water tank (or on demand water heaters), a gas refrigerator, a gas stove, a gas clothes dryer and even gas lighting.

They also tend to be the most affordable retail fuels. So long as you have a reliable source of propane or natural gas delivery, this is the most comfortable and efficient way to go. Heating (including cooking and heating water) is the worst waste of electricity, and superior results can be obtained by using the heat by-product of burning gas.

Battery Banks

One way to reduce the need for burning fuel by running a generator constantly is using deep cycle battery banks. The cost was prohibitive to us, but the basic idea is that you get as many heavy duty, high quality, AGM deep cycle batteries as you can afford, connect them with an intelligent charger system to a heavy-duty battery charger that is connected to the generator power and a good quality inverter that will convert the battery power to regular household power. The batteries act as electrical storage devices to power your home in between generator sessions.

A Side Note About Inverters

There are a lot of discussions online about sine wave inverters, which are expensive but provide clean power similar to the power company's AC power, vs. modified sine wave inverters, which are cheaper but accused of providing "dirty" power that's "bad" for any motors or electronics on that circuit. We did not experience any problems with our precious electronics from the modified inverter in our Noma Powerpack, but it wasn't powerful enough to run many motors.

Wood Stove

We like the idea of a wood stove so much that we bought a used one when we first moved in for $100 including delivery, chimney pipe not included (more on that in a moment).

We had one in our previous home and it was fantastic to have even with the power on, when it provides toasty, cozy, supplemental heat, but especially during power outages when it provides essential heating and the ability to boil water and cook or reheat food.

The insurance company has a few rules for installing a wood stove, such as the distance between it and the walls and the use of insulating materials underneath and behind it, but they are quite affordable and easy to install.

However, there is one surprisingly daunting aspect to installing a wood stove in the home which has stopped us in our tracks, even still, at least until we figure a way to do it, and that's the chimney.

The price of a new modest chimney kit is over $2,000. Since we plan to put ours through the wall and run it up the side of the house it will be mostly exposed to the elements, which limits its life expectancy to about 15 years. Or so they say... we have never actually heard of anyone replacing their wood stove chimney as a matter of routine maintenance before, and this might just be fine print on the part of the manufacturers, but it still makes such a large purchase even more daunting.

We live in a rural part of Canada, and many older homes here use wood heat, so we thought surely there must be affordable used chimneys available. This has not turned out to be the case. We even set up an ad watch for the local online classifieds and have been monitoring it for several years now. A "good deal" is something along the lines of $500 plus the labor to take it down and remove it, for old, weather-worn, rusty, sometimes dented chimney pipe. We're pretty handy when it comes to a lot of things, but we don't do roofs, as there's too much risk of injury from a fall. We have to protect ourselves since as freelance workers, we don't qualify for worker's compensation or paid leave, so we have to factor in the costs of de-installation, then re-installation by professionals. The high cost of even a used chimney has prevented us from installing this useful, even essential, off-grid home heating appliance.

We sure miss the wood stove we had in our last home! Compared to the five minutes of heat that a furnace blows on each cycle, a wood stove generates a nice constant heat that feels much cozier and toastier than anything else.

As mentioned earlier, it's easy to imagine the previous owners of our old farmhouse excitedly making the big switch from the traditional wood stove to a brand new, automatic, electric, forced-air furnace. Clean heat pumped through ducts evenly into every room of the house. No more getting up in the middle of the night to feed the wood stove. No more chopping and carrying wood. No more ashes to clean out.

How sad that this meant the house would never be as warm again, and would be susceptible to freezing during even minor winter storms that happen to cause a power outage. There's no way to even cook up a tea or warm up some leftovers. For a home that was built in the 1850s to be completely self-sufficient, before anyone had even imagined a "power-grid," it's a tragic reliance on the circumstantial reliability of that grid.

Water Tanks

It's possible to install a large freshwater holding tank next to your deep well jet pump and connect it with a switch to ensure it's always topped up every time the generator runs. We even considered re-purposing our electric hot water tank for cold water storage. Then, you can connect the cold water holding tank to your household water supply system with a small, 12V (battery powered) electric pump and a pressure tank. It doesn't take much power to pressurize the system and will cause far less drain on your battery bank than running a jet pump 100 feet or more down a well every time you turn on a water tap.

You can heat your household water system with on-demand water heaters that run on propane or natural gas. They are surprisingly affordable and efficient.

We have a family member who lives in a small two-room shack in the snowy mountains of rural Canada. He does not have electricity but he has a wood stove and a hand-operated (lever style) water pump. These two things are all you need to survive off-grid. If you have these and a generator, you're doing great!

Now picture yourself adding a few solar panels here and there to supplement your lighting, computer use, etc. and you can see how you might continue to build on to your little off-grid world, adding individual solutions for each new need that arises.

Solar panels

Power grid electricity conveniently takes care of many needs for us with one easy solution, but this convenience is not a necessity and it's replaceable with a bit of imagination and determination.

Human Power

There are a lot of great people-powered appliances out there like wind-up flashlights, but much bigger pedal powered units. There are even ways to make your own with a bicycle on a stationary stand, with a belt around the back wheel connected to a car alternator. Hey, if you can get your workout and it pays for your internet time that sounds good to us!

Hybrid Off-Grid

Another compelling option to consider is taking your on-grid house off-grid temporarily. This means that you choose to be off-grid powering everything with solar when the sun shines (or wind power when the wind blows), but when you're short on power (like on laundry day), you go back on-grid and use utility power. This gives you the best of both worlds and a reliable backup both ways.

Chapter 14
Conclusion

Although we decided to go back on-grid after one year, we don't want to discourage anyone who may be considering the off-grid lifestyle. We did not give up on it, it just became obvious to us that to do it comfortably and in a sustainable way would require a huge investment, largely in solar. Solar is not the only way, but for now, there's nothing else that offers that kind of freedom in the off-grid lifestyle.

We made a nice sum of money on one of our larger jobs, and the question was: Do we update and repair our old farmhouse's electrical problem so we can live in it "normally," on-grid again, or do we invest the same money in going "all in" on the various off-grid options, like solar panels, AGM batteries, an extra generator and propane heating?

We decided that we wanted our old farmhouse to get "proper" electricity service again. Given that our farmhouse was built before electricity was even available, it's interesting to ask ourselves, "How did those folks live back then, in this same old house, which had no electricity to begin with?"

If you decide to do this, it will be hard in many ways. It is more inconvenient than anything, but many conveniences are a matter of habit. Ultimately, we found that there are only two things a family needs to survive. Those two things were most likely originally installed in our house but have been removed over time. The two things you need to survive are:

- A wood stove

- A non-electrical water source (town water, lake or river, etc.) or a hand pump to pull water from a well

That's it.

Hand-operated water pump

We did not have these essential things when we were off-grid, but if you do, you're in a good position to go off-grid permanently. You do not need much else if you don't care about modern luxuries like appliances.

There are many more conveniences that we discussed in this book, as most likely you are not trying to live like a mountain man (or woman) out in a little cabin in the woods with just your wood stove and water source. You probably would like some internet and a few other modern necessities, so we've tried to help in every way we can with information that hopefully you have found relevant and interesting.

We have tried to find the point where comfort meets necessity with regard to survival. We were not always as comfortable as we wanted to be, but sometimes a bit of sacrifice can yield great results. This experience taught us quite a few lessons about many aspects of life. Now that the book is finished, I can look back and say that the whole experience was worthwhile and one I would wholeheartedly endorse, even if for a short while.

We've been continuously inspired by the many off-grid and camper van nomads out there living with the bare necessities. Before we found ourselves serendipitously off-grid, we were researching camper vans and how to live in them for extended periods.

The funny thing was that we were spending a lot of time researching the off-grid lifestyle and had gathered a lot of information from watching those brave camper people... and then our power went out, and it became real, fast!

Your Reasons for Wanting to Go Off-Grid

I know there are many reasons to want to go off-grid. I read a story about a family of four who lived out of their truck camper and home-schooled their children. Because they had decided to live this way, they had toured a lot of places and the children had seen a lot of great sights. They said that because there was not a lot of room in their little home, there was not a lot of room for bickering!

Whatever your reasons, I hope this book will give you some new (or old, as in the case of a wood stove) insights into what's to be learned from going off-grid and being better prepared in case of a long-term power outage.

Thank you so much for reading this book. I hope you enjoyed it and learned something useful.

Good luck!

If you've enjoyed reading this book, subscribe* to my mailing list for exclusive content and sneak peaks of my future books.

Visit the link below:

http://eepurl.com/glvBjj

OR

Use the QR Code:

(*Must be 13 years or older to subscribe)

Made in the USA
Middletown, DE
23 August 2019